YOU
ONLY HAVE
TO BE RIGHT
ONCE

YOU
ONLY HAVE
TO BE RIGHT
ONCE

The Unprecedented Rise of the
Instant Tech Billionaires

Randall Lane
and the staff of
Forbes

PORTFOLIO
PENGUIN

PORTFOLIO PENGUIN

Published by the Penguin Group
Penguin Books Ltd, 80 Strand, London WC2R 0RL, England
Penguin Group (USA) Inc., 375 Hudson Street, New York, New York 10014, USA
Penguin Group (Canada), 90 Eglinton Avenue East, Suite 700, Toronto, Ontario, Canada M4P 2Y3
(a division of Pearson Penguin Canada Inc.)
Penguin Ireland, 25 St Stephen's Green, Dublin 2, Ireland (a division of Penguin Books Ltd)
Penguin Group (Australia), 707 Collins Street, Melbourne, Victoria 3008, Australia
(a division of Pearson Australia Group Pty)
Penguin Books India Pvt Ltd, 11 Community Centre, Panchsheel Park, New Delhi – 110 017, India
Penguin Group (NZ), 67 Apollo Drive, Rosedale, Auckland 0632, New Zealand
(a division of Pearson New Zealand Ltd)
Penguin Books (South Africa) (Pty) Ltd, Block D, Rosebank Office Park,
181 Jan Smuts Avenue, Parktown North, Gauteng 2193, South Africa

Penguin Books Ltd, Registered Offices: 80 Strand, London WC2R 0RL, England

www.penguin.com

First published in the United States of America by Portfolio/Penguin,
a member of Penguin Group (USA) LLC 2014
First published in Great Britain by Portfolio Penguin 2014
001

Copyright © Forbes Media LLC, 2014
All rights reserved

The moral right of the copyright holder has been asserted

Most of the selections in this book have appeared in issues of *Forbes* magazine.

Photograph credits
Insert page 1 (top and bottom), 3 (top), 4 (top): Forbes Media LLC
2 (top): Elon Musk by Kristoffer Tripplaar/Alamy
2 (bottom): Christian Peacock
3 (bottom): Michele Clement
4 (bottom): Walter Smith
5 (top and bottom), 6 (top): © Eric Millette
6 (bottom): Don Feria/Getty Images
7 (top): © MGPI/MichaelGrecco.com
7 (bottom): Ethan Pines/Copyright © 2014 Ethan Pines
8 (top): Jamel Toppin
8 (bottom): Gabriela Hasbun

Printed in England by Clays Ltd, St Ives plc

ISBN: 978–0–241–18299–4

www.greenpenguin.co.uk

Penguin Books is committed to a sustainable
future for our business, our readers and our planet.
This book is made from Forest Stewardship
Council™ certified paper.

Contents

CONTENTS

Introduction

Wedged into a corner, Sean Parker sported the removed look of someone at a crowded party where they don't know many people. Which, at a media soiree at New York's clubby Monkey Bar on October 4, 2011, happened to be the case. Given that two weeks prior, Parker became the first person to adorn the cover of *Forbes* magazine since I returned as the editor, it seemed right to introduce myself.

"I know exactly who you are," Parker responded, quickly parrying with a short history of my personal background, *Forbes*'s position in the marketplace, and my stated goals for the magazine. He then explained his (typical) obsessiveness with a soliloquy that can be summed up in two words: *Thank you*.

It's not that the *Forbes* cover had been a valentine: It revealed the polymath who had helped shape Napster, Facebook, and Spotify with all his quirks and faults. But until that story—viewed more than 700,000 times online and by millions more who saw the print magazine version—the world equated him with the villainous character portrayed by Justin Timberlake in David Fincher's movie *The Social Network*. Even Mark Zuckerberg conceded the movie did Parker factual injustice. Reduced to an evil-businessman caricature,

Parker had barricaded himself in LA's Peninsula Hotel for two months, where he'd gained thirty pounds.

His twenty-two-year-old fiancée had helped him ditch the depression, and the weight. And so Parker stood before me, himself again, as a brash actor in a story that has only a little to do with Facebook and feels one hundred times bigger: how a handful of young digital swashbucklers shrugged off the Great Recession to transform how industries operate and fortunes get made.

The day after my conversation with Parker, Steve Jobs passed away. Jobs had epitomized the *old* new guard, one of a trinity of tech entrepreneurs—with Bill Gates and Michael Dell—who two generations earlier, while themselves in their twenties, proved the disruptive power of technology. Now Jobs was dead. Gates had become a full-time philanthropist. And Dell's company, as with Apple and Microsoft, was viewed by this new generation as the bloated prey rather than the hungry predator.

This narrative isn't new. The first half century of the American computer age has seen perennial waves of the young taking on the old. During my first go-around at *Forbes*, just out of college in the early nineties, I chronicled tech-savvy Generation X, which valued entrepreneurship over the corporate ladder and fueled the original dotcom boom and bust, carving out a handful of huge winners, notably Google and eBay, in the process.

In this round, however, the underlying drivers have accelerated exponentially. This new model of Young Turk isn't merely comfortable with technology—he can't remember a world without the Internet. Accordingly, he's no longer content merely conquering the technology space—*every* industry is now the technology space, whether hotels or music or transportation. And thus ripe for pillaging.

Then there's the cash. History will determine whether this proves to be yet another financial bubble—when a five-year-old taxi-sharing app, Uber, raises venture money at a $17 billion valuation, it's hard to bet against that. But what's undeniable is that we're witnessing the most prodigious wealth machine in human history. Zuckerberg, worth some $30 billion on his thirtieth birthday, may be the poster boy for this new breed, but he's far from an outlier. Almost a dozen Americans, ineligible by dint of age to serve as president, became self-made billionaires over the past five years. What's more, no one in this cohort finds that particularly unusual—they pretty much feel *entitled* to it.

Youth, meanwhile, has officially ceased to be a disadvantage, up-ending pretty much the entirety of civilized history. Previously, whether you were a blacksmith or a lawyer, wisdom and experience rendered you more valuable as years went on. No longer. For the past twenty years, if your computer broke, you'd prefer that the twenty-five-year-old fix it rather than the fifty-five-year-old. For ten years, venture capitalists favored young "digital natives" over industry vet-erans, as long as the former got paired with an operational "adult." We've now skipped the adult requirement. The kids are fully run-ning the show.

And unlike the hedge fund managers of the previous decade, who were rightly perceived to have conjured their billions without actually creating anything (other than the complicated financial structures that wound up collapsing everything else), no one resents them for it. Quite the contrary, they glide across the country in their chartered Gulfstreams like folk heroes.

The white hats stem from the perception of meritocracy. The high stakes put a premium on ideas and technical execution, rather than connections and salesmanship. As you turn the pages of this book, there's a far higher correlation between financial success and a stint as a teen hacker than having daddy's name on a building at Harvard. The engineers have trumped the salesmen. Sexism remains embedded in the coder-boy set (it's not by choice that this book is chock-a-block with guys; very few women have launched major tech-enabled start-ups). But just ask Jan Koum or Pejman Nozad or Daniel Ek—the American Dream has never been more vivid. The only nepotism, as best as I can tell, comes from being the catalyst's roommate, buddy, or frat brother. (In the 2010s, there's no sweeter title than "co-founder.") It's hard to resent someone when you had the same shot at the brass ring.

To me, however, the ultimate commonality across all these chapters, the one that lets them reap adulation, boils down to individualism. The post-meltdown recovery has proven among the most tepid in national history, especially the job market. Where others see a paralysis-inducing world, these guys see a gold rush, and they *take action*. They'd all rather regret the things they did than what they didn't do. Jobs and Gates and Dell made dropping out acceptable; among this group, it's cool, a badge of honor. (Snapchat's Evan Spiegel dropped out of Stanford in the middle of a class, a month before graduation . . . on principle.)

Failure is an acceptable option. There's hardly anyone in this book who hasn't tasted it. Venture capitalists, in fact, view failure as an asset, and fund based on whether you've had the good fortune to make mistakes on someone else's dime. The entire VC ecosystem is based on flops: the idea that a one-in-ten success ratio is fine, as long as that success is a blockbuster. *You only have to be right once.* The greatest successes come when people aren't afraid to fail—a decidedly American outlook that explains why almost every innovation of the Internet era has sprung from this country.

Credit belongs to the *Forbes* writers and researchers who brought forward—and home—this endless parade of digital robber barons: George Anders, Victoria Barrett, Jeff Bercovici, Steve Bertoni, Abram Brown, J. J. Colao, Hannah Elliott, David Ewalt, Tomio Geron, Andy Greenberg, Ryan Mac, Parmy Olson, and Eric Savitz. This book, to a large degree, is yours. Thanks at Penguin's Portfolio imprint go to Adrian Zackheim, Natalie Horbachevsky, and Will Weisser, who instantly grasped the power and importance of what we'd assembled, and scrambled with the speed of a start-up to get this to market. At *Forbes,* two people deserve a special call-out: Lewis D'Vorkin, *Forbes*'s chief product officer, whose return to *Forbes* four years ago brought a refocus on chronicling people-based entrepreneurial capitalism—he set the stage for the stories that infuse this book; and Bruce Upbin, who as managing editor oversees *Forbes*'s technology coverage—he was at the genesis of almost all of these profiles.

For the past three years, my job has provided the perfect perch to see the waves swell, as *Forbes*, scorekeepers of capitalism, emerged as the preferred venue to introduce (or reintroduce) yourself to the world. The large majority of these chapters were born from *Forbes* magazine features, and the majority of those were cover stories. The facts in every chapter have been updated, resulting in an accurate snapshot of what was going on as we went to press in the summer of 2014. I ordered them in roughly sequential order, based on when the companies began taking off. Even across just three years of profiles, while the core traits remain consistent, you'll see the numbers swell ever-larger.

Which brings us back to my party pal Sean Parker. The most famous line attributed to him in *The Social Network*, of course, was his advice to Zuckerberg on their first meeting: *A million dollars isn't cool. You know what's cool? A billion dollars.* It was, he told me, complete Hollywood fiction. He never said it. And even if he had, as you progress though these chapters, you'll recognize a second level of folly. In the land of the young tech elite, a billion isn't cool anymore. Ten billion is.

—Randall Lane, August 2014

@RandallLane

YOU
ONLY HAVE
TO BE RIGHT
ONCE

CHAPTER 1

Sean Parker, Facebook: Master of Disruption

The evolution of the Internet, from unfettered hacker toy to unlimited wealth machine, comes embodied in one Sean Parker. As the teenage cofounder of Napster, the music piracy site that nearly crippled the recording industry, he gained notoriety, even as he flirted with bankruptcy and jail. As the twentysomething president of Facebook, entrusted with giving Mark Zuckerberg some adult supervision, he cemented his digital bad boy reputation, even as he made himself a few billion dollars. But when **Steven Bertoni** tried to track down the mercurial Parker in 2011, he found proof of the adage about wealth's ability to buy happiness. Parker, recovering from surgery and a freshly branded villain of the tech world, courtesy of David Fincher's movie *The Social Network,* devolved into a hermit, holing up in the Peninsula Hotel in Los Angeles for two months, a digital Howard Hughes. When he emerged, he invited Bertoni for what was supposed to be a relatively brief sit-down in his new $20 million town-house in New York's Greenwich Village. That meeting turned into a meticulously chosen sushi dinner, and after two bottles of expensive sake, a trip to the West Coast, via rented Gulfstream, where Parker pinballed around various interests. His passion at the time: Airtime, a video-sharing service that he zealously kept under wraps—and eventually flopped. No big deal. This is a guy adept at identifying problems, and at peace if not every solution works out. He also backed Spotify, a legal reincarnation of Napster—by 2014, it was valued at more than $4 billion.

Pointed toward his eighteen-acre compound in Marin County, Sean Parker ripped through the night fog on the Golden Gate Bridge in a stealthy Audi S6 that masks a Lamborghini engine, one pale hand on the wheel, the other toggling through thousands of songs uploaded on the car's sound system.

Facebook's former president had endured a typically busy day. Over the last ten hours he'd interviewed two potential VPs for his new video startup, answered hours' worth of e-mails about the music platform he was backing, Spotify, and met with a potential CEO for his Facebook charity app, Causes. He had also booked bands and wrangled vendors for his engagement party, scheduled in New Jersey the same night Hurricane Irene hammered the Northeast (with Lenny Kravitz grounded in North Carolina, he eventually subbed in the Cold War Kids). Later, he broke from work to dine with Jack Dorsey, the chief of Facebook rival Twitter and payment service

Square. After dinner, at the restaurant bar, he interviewed another potential boss for Causes. By the time he dropped me off at my hotel, it was 11:30 p.m. Parker's day was about half done.

For the next six hours Parker fired off e-mails, then turned to his private Facebook page. The previous afternoon—or earlier the same day, if you're on Parker's body clock—the world had learned that Steve Jobs resigned from Apple. Around 6:00 a.m., Parker posted this Schopenhauer quote: "We can come to look upon the deaths of our enemies with as much regret as we feel for those of our friends, namely, when we miss their existence as witnesses to our success." It immediately leaked. Gossip site Gawker accused him of dancing on Jobs's grave. He e-mailed Gawker that the quote was a tribute to Jobs—his longtime idol and more recent rival (iTunes versus Spotify). Just before 7:00 a.m. he went to bed.

Four hours later he was up, ready to do it all again.

Flighty, manic, and unpredictable, Parker grates on investors— he's been jettisoned from the three companies he helped create, soon after they lifted off. "He's seen as an unknown quantity, and VCs love for things to be very much in control," said Facebook cofounder Dustin Moskovitz. But VCs also love big ideas, and Parker has those in spades—LinkedIn founder Reid Hoffman calls him a "big-ass visionary." And in terms of boardroom scheming, he's nothing like his fictional portrayal in *The Social Network*. "The movie needed an antagonist, but that's not what he was," said former Facebook growth chief Chamath Palihapitiya. "He's really the exact opposite of his portrayal in the film."

Boiled down, Sean Parker is a human accelerant, an idea catalyst who, when combined with the right people, has fueled some of the most disruptive companies of the last two decades. At just nineteen he blew up the record industry as the cofounder of the music-sharing site Napster. Two years later his address book service, Plaxo, demonstrated the potency of digital propagation, something he took a step further as the twenty-four-year-old president of Facebook, helping the social network become the most important Internet company since, well, maybe ever. Yes, all three companies eventually bounced him, but not before, by thirty-one, he tucked away enough equity to boast a fortune of more than $2 billion. And he was just getting started.

By 2011 he was out to upend music distribution again, bringing the Swedish music platform Spotify to America—and masterminding how the service would work with Facebook's music efforts. He was also hunting new startups as general partner at venture firm Founders Fund and reuniting with Napster's Shawn Fanning to create Airtime, a live video site.

Parker's personal network is astounding, a combination of foresight and fate. Starting as a teenager, when he interned for Mark Pincus (now Zynga's chairman) Parker has teamed, in one way or another, with the men who now control the modern Internet: Mark Zuckerberg, Mike Moritz, Peter Thiel, Reid Hoffman, Yuri Milner, Dustin Moskovitz, Adam D'Angelo, Daniel Ek, Ron Conway, Ram Shriram, and Jim Breyer.

"He can see things most people won't be able to see for a year or two," said Palihapitiya. As Shervin Pishevar of Menlo Ventures describes it: "Parker has access to trends and signals that are invisible to many people. For him it's like hearing a dog whistle." Parker didn't disagree: "I find a lot of things relevant that aren't necessarily relevant to the world when I'm thinking about them." Parker is drawn to big, universal problems and spends years looking for them.

"Most of us kind of agree on the thrust of history. The key is to understand how we get there," said the young billionaire as he rolled his desk chair closer to me in the office of his recently purchased $20 million Manhattan townhouse. "The transition strategies are more important than understanding what the outcome state will be."

By focusing on problem selection, rather than rushing out an innovation no one wants, like so many trigger-happy entrepreneurs, Parker put himself in position for the string of blockbusters that his critics blithely attribute to sequential luck. Napster was the transition between CDs and MP3s after the Internet made it possible to strip content from its container. Facebook was a vehicle to create a reliable identity in an anonymous online world. Spotify is an attempt to fix the very music industry that Napster helped break a decade before.

"He thinks about where he perceives the world to be going," explained Spotify founder Daniel Ek. "If he doesn't think there is a company that will win, then he builds it himself."

This deep investigative thinking bleeds into everything else in his life. Ask Parker about the genesis of his former company Plaxo, and he starts with theories of how real viruses spread across populations. Before he shares the name of his favorite sushi restaurant— prior to one dinner we had in New York, he called five to find out which chef was cutting the fish that night—he discusses rice density and the ideal geometric shape for sushi cuts (trapezoids). Question this audiophile about the best brand of headphones and you first learn how sound waves are registered by our tympanic membranes. As the expression goes, ask him for the time, and he'll tell you how to build a watch.

"We talked for what I originally scheduled for an hour, ended up being three hours," Reid Hoffman recalled about their first meeting back in 2002. Jack Dorsey had the same experience: "It's rare to find someone who can have those kinds of conversations. . . . I appreciate any conversation where I can walk away questioning myself and my ideas."

Thus, Parker's life becomes impervious to time, a subject friends and business partners acknowledge with a defeated laugh. Peter Thiel calls it Parker's "absence of dramatic punctuality." Ek manages Parker by telling him there's a meeting at 11:00 a.m. and informing others it starts at 1:00 p.m. There's even a name in Silicon Valley for this phenomenon: Sean Standard Time.

"Making people wait and not fulfilling all your obligations feels bad. I probably feel worse about it than people realize, but I don't do it with malice," said Parker. When focused on a task, he blocks everything else out and works himself into a trance. The outside world fades; time slips away. "It requires a lot of rescheduling, but I try to focus on things that are the highest value and get those done perfectly."

Parker's definition of "done perfectly" is extreme. On the afternoon of his *Forbes* cover shoot, Parker summoned three full racks of Italian suits. Twenty dress shirts—still in their wrappings—waited on the wicker couch in his Greenwich Village townhouse. Rows of eyeglasses and sunglasses blanketed the coffee table, piles of suspenders and ties filled chairs, a shoe store's worth of wingtips, loafers, and boots lined the wall. The shoot was scheduled for 4:00 p.m. Sean emerged at 5:30 p.m., flanked by a proper entourage: a clothes stylist, hairstylist, makeup artist, assistant, publicist, tailor, and his fiancée (now his wife), Alexandra Lenas.

During the shoot Parker changed his wardrobe more often than a Las Vegas headliner. He switched from streamlined suits to three-piece numbers to casual cardigans over designer jeans. He obsessed over the spacing of suspenders and triple-checked that the red in his skinny tie matched the red in his hipster eyeglasses. At one point he broke for a snack. Ten minutes later he was in the kitchen, dressed in a dark Christian Dior suit, whisking a bowl of homemade ranch dip. He was trying to lose weight and was eating only vegetables. The ranch dressing on hand was too runny, so he added sour cream to firm it up. His assistant (one of three) coaxed him back in front of the camera. After hundreds of photos in four locations around the house, the shoot was finished, at 2:00 a.m.—perfect, calibrated Sean Standard Time.

Two nights later I arrived at his house at 11:00 p.m. A chartered G450 was scheduled to fly to San Francisco from Teterboro, New Jersey—wheels up at midnight, sharp. Parker was out meeting Spotify's Ek. When midnight hit and there was still no Parker, I got a little nervous. Everyone else yawned. Parker strutted in at 2:00 a.m. He still had to pack and shower. At 3:30 a.m. a Cadillac Escalade was loaded with luggage and takeout fried chicken from Blue Ribbon, a late-night, New York chefs' hangout, and across the Hudson we went.

We took off at 4:00 a.m., a half hour before FAA fatigue laws would have grounded the pilots. When I awoke to a view of the California desert outside the plane window, Parker was sitting across from me, snacking on a piece of fried chicken, his veggie-only diet already over. "Did you sleep well?"

We landed in San Francisco at 9:00 a.m., where yet another Escalade ferried us to Marin County. Everyone parted ways to sleep for a few more hours before Parker, eager to meet with colleagues and pitch potential hires, began a sprint through San Francisco and Silicon Valley.

PARKER'S PATH TO SILICON Valley began the day his father, Bruce, formerly the chief scientist at the National Oceanic and Atmospheric Administration, taught him how to program on an Atari 800. He was in second grade. By high school Parker was hacking into companies and universities (alias: dob, which he chose for its aesthetic symmetry). When he was fifteen, his hacking caught the attention of the FBI, earning him community service. At sixteen he won the Virginia state computer science fair for developing an early Web crawler and was recruited by the CIA. Instead he interned for Mark Pincus's D.C. startup, Free-Loader, and then UUNET, an early Internet service provider. "I wasn't going to school," he said. "I was technically in a co-op program but in truth was just going to work." Parker made $80,000 his senior year, enough to convince his parents to let him put off college and join Shawn Fanning, a teenager he'd met on a dial-up bulletin board, to start a music-sharing site, which became Napster in 1999.

Parker never did make it to college, but Napster provided an education all its own. "I kind of refer to it as Napster University—it was a crash course in intellectual property law, corporate finance, entrepreneurship, and law school," said Parker. "Some of the e-mails I wrote when I was just a kid who didn't know what he was doing are apparently in [law school] textbooks." Those e-mails, which admitted Napster customers were likely stealing music, would end up as evidence in copyright lawsuits that would eventually shutter Napster. But by that time Parker had already been exiled by management and was living in a North Carolina beach house. "I didn't understand at the time that when someone asks you to take an extended vacation that's basically a prelude to firing you."

While at Napster, Parker met angel investor Ron Conway, who was funding another company in the startup's building in Santa Clara. Conway has backed every Parker production since.

On our first night in San Francisco, Parker and I visited Conway on the porch of his house overlooking Richardson Bay. We drank Brunello and nibbled on prosciutto. "We've gone through hell together," said Conway, who backed Google, PayPal, Twitter, and FourSquare, among others.

Napster was less a company than an all-hours circus, a strange tangle of people who thought they had joined a renegade social movement rather than a startup. "So much of what I learned at Napster was learning what not to do," said Parker, as Conway scribbled on a notepad. Conway had learned the hard way to listen to Parker. "When Sean became president of Facebook, he called me and said, 'You have to look at this company.' The killer is that I could have been Peter Thiel," said Conway, referring to Thiel's investment in Facebook, which made him a billionaire. "But I said, 'You have to clean up the issues at Plaxo, so don't introduce me to this Facebook thing.'" He sipped his wine, shook his head and laughed: "These are painful memories."

Plaxo was Parker's first attempt at creating a real company—an online service that aimed to keep your address book up to date. It sounds boring compared to Napster and Facebook, but Plaxo was an early social networking tool and a pioneer of the types of viral tricks that helped grow LinkedIn, Zynga, and Facebook. "Plaxo is like the indie band that the public doesn't know but was really influential with other musicians," said Parker.

Once you downloaded Plaxo, the program would mine your address book and e-mail every contact with a message, coaxing them to sign up for the service. When the next person signed up, the software would pirate the new address book and spread further. Within a short time millions of e-mail accounts had been hit with Plaxo pitches. "In some ways, Plaxo is the company I'm most proud of because it was the company that wreaked the most havoc on the world," said Parker. Those experiences later changed the history of Facebook.

There are diverging stories about Parker's swift exile from Plaxo. His take is that Ram Shriram, a former Google board member recruited to help manage the company, conspired to throw him out and strip him of his stock. "Ram Shriram played this very vindictive game not only to force me out of the company but force me out broke, penniless, impoverished, and with no options."

Shriram would not speak about this, but cofounders Todd Masonis and Cameron Ring shared a different story: that Parker was essential in creating the company strategy and raising money but grew bored with the daily grind of running it. Masonis claimed that Parker was often absent, and when he was around, he was distracting: "It was the sort of thing where he doesn't come to work, but then maybe if he does it's at 11:00 p.m., but it's not to do a bunch of work, it's because he's bringing a bunch of girls back to the office because he can show them he's a startup founder."

Whatever the motivation, Parker's removal was messy. He insisted that investors had hired a private eye to build a case. There were allegations of misconduct and drug use—claims that went unproven. "It happened poorly; we should have done a better job being up front about it and doing it ourselves," said Ring. "But looking back, it was the right decision for us and for Sean."

Parker was on his own, isolated from his cofounders and close friends. "I felt a complete loss of faith in humanity, impending doom, a sense that I couldn't trust anybody," said Parker. He thought of suing but knew the battle could drag on for years. So he let it go. After all, he had already discovered a new company with potential to get really big.

WHEN PARKER WAS FIRST shown Facebook by a friend's girlfriend (not through a one-night stand, as depicted in Aaron Sorkin's screenplay) he was already a social networking veteran, both because of Plaxo and, more directly, as an advisor to Friendster, the ill-fated Facebook forerunner he stumbled across when reporters asked him if it was connected to the similar-sounding Napster. He knew the larger college market was ripe for its own social network—there were several small sites functioning at individual universities—and Facebook, which had already leapt off Harvard's campus, gave him a play. He wrote to Facebook's generic e-mail address and later met Zuckerberg and Eduardo Saverin over a Chinese dinner in Manhattan in the spring of 2004.

A few weeks later, by chance, he ran into Zuckerberg and crew on the streets of Palo Alto and shortly moved into Dustin Moskovitz's room at the rented Facebook house. "It's the only thing the movie got kind of close to right," deadpanned Adam D'Angelo, Facebook's early technology chief, whom I met at the Palo Alto headquarters of his company, question-and-answer site Quora.

Just twenty-four, Parker was Facebook's business veteran. He helped the college-aged Facebook founders network around Silicon Valley, set up routers, and meet benevolent investors like Thiel, Hoffman, and Pincus.

"Sean was pivotal in helping Facebook transform from a college project into a real company," Mark Zuckerberg said in an e-mail. "Perhaps more importantly, Sean helped ensure that anyone interested in investing in Facebook would not only buy into a company, but also a mission and vision of making the world more open through sharing."

D'Angelo credited Parker for recognizing that design was as vital as engineering. "Our first employee [at Quora] was a designer, and we knew to do that because we saw how important that was at Facebook." Together with Aaron Sittig, an early Napster friend who would become Facebook's key architect, Parker helped drive Facebook's minimalist look. He was adamant that the site should have a continuous flow and that tasks like adding friends be as frictionless as possible. "We wanted it to be like a telephone service," said Sittig. "Something that really fades into the background." Later Parker helped push Facebook's photo-sharing function. It would be one of his last acts as Facebook's president.

In August 2005, Parker was questioned in North Carolina after cops found cocaine in a beach house rented under his name. He was never arrested or charged, but the incident swiftly kick-started his downfall at Facebook.

Because of agreements, the principals can't discuss how or why he was ousted. The Team Parker take was that Accel Partners resented him because he forced the VC to invest in Facebook at a then-high $100 million valuation (Accel has since invested in Spotify, and its star Jim Breyer now says Parker had "exceptional insight"). Parker had many supporters, and the cocaine controversy caused a rift between the founders and the investors. In the end, Parker decided it was best for Facebook if he resigned. He had been pushed out of his third company in five years. He moved to New York in the fall of 2005, crashing with Grateful Dead lyricist John Perry Barlow, a friend from the Napster days.

Although no longer on the Facebook payroll, Parker continued to advise Zuckerberg on strategy and to recruit key executives like Chamath Palihapitiya. Sittig said he still helped with the site's design and was a strong outside influence in the development of Facebook's "share" platform, which allowed users to upload news articles, video, and other third-party content. Still, likely Parker's greatest contribution to Facebook was his creation of a corporate structure—based on his Plaxo experience—that gave Zuckerberg complete and permanent control of the company he founded.

Parker's plan fortified Zuckerberg with supervoting shares that resisted dilution during fundraising and armed him with enough board seats to stay in power for as long as he wanted. "Sean was pretty material in setting up the company in a way that Mark retained as much control as he does, both in being able to get high-valuation, low-dilution financing but also in terms of the board structure itself and details of control," said Facebook cofounder Dustin Moskovitz. "He'd been coming off the Plaxo mess and was sensitive to that."

This is what made his portrayal in *The Social Network* so frustrating to Parker. Justin Timberlake's Parker is a cruel, cocky opportunist who forces Eduardo Saverin out of the company and robs him of his shares. At Plaxo, Parker had endured in real life what the fictional Saverin suffered in the film. "I don't mind being depicted as a decadent partyer, because I don't think there's anything morally wrong with that," said Parker, quickly adding that the partying was exaggerated, too. "But I do mind being depicted as an unethical, mercenary operator, because I do think there is something wrong with that."

The movie debuted in October 2010 to critical and commercial success. It cut Parker deep. "I was a mess at that point because the movie had hit, the depiction of me was so far from reality I was having a hard time psychologically dealing with it," Parker said. "I was all bummed out, I had just broken up with my girlfriend of four years and I just had knee surgery, so I couldn't walk." Before the film's release he laid up in a suite at the Peninsula Hotel in L.A. for two months. He gained thirty pounds. He was also juggling his duties at Founders Fund, Spotify, and startup Airtime.

It got to be too much. He took a break from Airtime, his knee healed, and a mutual friend introduced him to his future wife, the twenty-two-year-old Lenas, a singer-songwriter.

FOR ALL THAT HE has accomplished, Parker remains a hacker at heart, motivated less by money—though Facebook's IPO catapulted his net worth, by mid-2014, toward $3 billion—than the drive to disrupt. Hence, he has never stopped thinking about Napster. In 2010, eight years after Napster had been sued out of existence, Parker was still searching for a company that could fulfill its promise of sharing music, but this time in a way that would pay the musicians, too. Like Facebook's photo sharing, he envisioned that music would thrive on the social graph. He just needed a vehicle to share the songs on Facebook.

Two years before, a friend had told him about a Swedish music site called Spotify that offered unlimited, legal songs. He scoured his network for an introduction, and without seeing the product in action, blindly e-mailed founder Daniel Ek, outlining his ideal music platform, hoping Spotify fit the description.

Ek had been a huge fan of Napster, and Parker's suggestions caught his attention: "This was someone who had spent more time thinking about this than I had done myself." After a series of e-mails and a test drive of the platform, Parker was sold and tried to invest. Armed with a cash infusion from Hong Kong billionaire Li Ka-shing, Ek wasn't looking for any more. Parker would have to prove his way into the company. He introduced Spotify to Mark Zuckerberg (a Facebook integration plan followed) and helped open doors at Warner and Universal, winning over Spotify's board: Parker eventually invested about $30 million.

In 2012, Parker also put money and effort into Airtime, a site where friends could post videos and react to them, which reunited him with his old Napster partner, Fanning. Parker had been coy about the platform's specifics, saying only that it would offer communication and sharing in real time—something he thought was underserved on the Web. "My pitch is eliminating loneliness," said Parker. Airtime included a random video chat function similar to 2010's voyeuristic flameout, the now-defunct Chatroulette. The ideas hit the same thread that has run through all of Parker's projects: sharing and discovery. (Unfortunately, like Chatroulette, Airtime flopped.)

These projects put him constantly on the road. He flew in a monthly loop from New York (base) to Los Angeles (music executives) to San Francisco (Founders Fund), then Stockholm and London (Spotify). It's a routine he still follows, albeit in slower rotation since the 2013 birth of his baby girl, Winter. In my last meeting with him I asked where he filed his taxes. "That's a damn good question. I don't even know."

Our get-together back at his New York town house started at 1:00 p.m. but went late. The next day, Parker was to fly to Stockholm to help the design team tweak the invitation process and shore up other features in time for the Spotify Facebook launch. "I need to go to the gym tonight, I got another hour's worth of e-mail, and I have to pack for my two-week European journey," he said, checking the clock on one of two computer screens on the desk. It's 3:00 a.m. "I actually couldn't honestly tell you whether we've been here for two hours or twenty minutes."

CHAPTER 2

Drew Houston, Dropbox:
No More Hot Pockets

The entirety of Drew Houston's business education came from fraternity life. If you're a preternatural coder, that's apparently now enough. As a student at MIT tired of eating microwaved Hot Pockets, Houston decided he wanted to start a company and get rich. He just needed an idea—which came to him while he was stuck on a bus with his laptop, with the data he needed parked on a different computer. Cloud-based file-sharing was soon available to the masses. When **Victoria Barret** caught up with Houston in late 2011, his four-year-old Dropbox was serving as the digital attic for 50 million people, storing their photos and files. Her *Forbes* cover story in late 2011 caused a sensation—more than a million people read the online post about the twenty-six-year-old suddenly worth $600 million on paper. And he was just getting started. Less than three years later, 300 million people use Dropbox. A huge, $325 million funding round in April 2014 gave him a war chest big enough to move into the enterprise market—and valued his company high enough ($9.5 billion) to give Houston, not yet thirty, a net worth of $1.4 billion. That will surely spike up further if the company, as anticipated, goes public in 2015. "I have to learn how to be big," Houston told Barret. Indeed.

———

Here's that rare Steve Jobs story, one that's never been told, about the company that got away. Jobs had been tracking a young software developer named Drew Houston, who blasted his way onto Apple's radar screen when he reverse-engineered Apple's file system so that his startup's logo, an unfolding box, appeared elegantly tucked inside. Not even an Apple SWAT team had been able to do that.

In December 2009 Jobs beckoned Houston (pronounced like the New York City street, not the Texas city) and his partner, Arash Ferdowsi, for a meeting at his Cupertino office. "I mean, Steve friggin' Jobs," remembered Houston. "How do you even prepare for that?" When Houston whipped out his laptop for a demo, Jobs, in his signature jeans and black turtleneck, coolly waved him away: "I know what you do."

What Houston does is Dropbox, the digital storage service that has surged to 275 million users, with another joining every second. Jobs presciently saw this sapling as a strategic asset for Apple. Houston cut Jobs' pitch short: He was determined to build a big company, he interjected, and wasn't selling, no matter the status of the bidder (Houston considered Jobs his hero) or the prospects of a nine-digit price (he and Ferdowsi drove to the meeting in a Zipcar Prius).

Jobs smiled warmly as he told them he was going after their market. "He said we were a feature, not a product," said Houston. Courteously, Jobs spent the next half hour waxing on over tea about his return to Apple, and why not to trust investors, as the duo—or more accurately, Houston, who plays Penn to Ferdowsi's mute Teller—peppered him with questions.

When Jobs later followed up with a suggestion to meet at Dropbox's San Francisco office, Houston proposed that they instead meet in Silicon Valley. "Why let the enemy get a taste?" he later shrugged cockily. Instead, Jobs went dark, resurfacing in June 2011, at his final keynote speech, where he unveiled iCloud, and specifically knocked Dropbox as a half-attempt to solve the Internet's messiest dilemma: How do you get all your files, from all your devices, into one place?

Houston's reaction was less cocky: "Oh, shit." The next day he shot a missive to his staff: "We have one of the fastest-growing companies in the world," it began. Then it featured a list of onetime meteors that fell to Earth: MySpace, Netscape, Palm, Yahoo.

Dropbox's ascent has been just as stunning. The 50-million-user figure for 2011 was up threefold from a year earlier, and the company has solved the "freemium" riddle: 96 percent of those pay nothing, yet the company was able to hit $50 million in revenue that year—enough, Houston said, to make it profitable. With only seventy staffers, mostly engineers, Dropbox grossed nearly three times more per employee than even the darling of business models, Google.

It got better. That 96 percent of nonpaying customers were throwing their stuff into Dropbox at such a pace that thousands of people each day blew through the free two gigabytes of storage, upgrading to fifty gigs for $10 a month or 100 gigs for $20. As we went over this math with Houston, pointing out that sales would double even if he didn't sign up another customer (indeed, in 2013, Dropbox reached approximately $200 million in revenue), he paused to garnish this lovely inevitability: "But we will sign up many, many customers." By mid-2014, Dropbox had 300 million users.

WHEN DROPBOX BECAME A verb ("Dropbox me"), Silicon Valley took keen notice. By 2008 Houston had raised $7.2 million—enough cash, given the company's robust economic model, to get it into the black. In August 2011, Houston decided to go for the kill. He invited seven of the Valley's elite venture firms to visit Dropbox's San Francisco digs over a four-day stretch, and asked them for offers by the following Tuesday.

Only one came back to him quickly. Just before midnight the eve offers were due, Dropbox's head of business development—a former venture capitalist—suggested Houston either delay the round or even pull it. Houston's reply: "We said Tuesday. It isn't Tuesday."

Sure enough, every firm came back interested the next morning. Houston eventually made a deal, which closed in September 2011, that included Index Ventures as lead, plus Sequoia, Greylock, Benchmark, Accel, Goldman Sachs, and RIT Capital Partners. Many stretched their deal definitions to get in. It's the stuff of instant Silicon Valley legend: While the soft market, and Houston's insistence on dealing only with platinum-plated VCs, crimped his valuation a bit, five-year-old Dropbox still raised a whopping $250 million on a $4 billion valuation. "This is the hot company," says one prominent investor who didn't get in. "Everyone wanted to be a part of it." Houston's estimated 15 percent stake was worth, on paper, $600 million.

Leaning back in an Aeron chair two weeks after the deal closed, across from a customized neon sign that reads "ITJUSTWORKS" with "just work" popping out in blue, Houston mused on what he would do with his new quarter-billion-dollar war chest. The single-room office on gritty Market Street would soon give way to an 8,500-square-foot spread with views of the Bay as the Dropbox staff swelled from 70 to 200, still an absurdly low number given the company's size. And Houston would see whether he could realize the vow he made to Jobs about building a major company, or else fall prey to the MySpace-esque hazards Jobs predicted. "I have to learn how to be big," he said.

IT WAS JUST BEFORE midnight on a Monday, and Houston turned his favorite late-night watering hole, the bar in San Francisco's W Hotel, into a fraternity party—literally. The first to arrive was Adam Smith, who was a fellow Phi Delta Theta at MIT before dropping out to start an e-mail search company, Xobni. Then came Chris, Jason, and Joe (who has a Dropbox tattoo on his arm because he feels "Drew is changing the world"), more MIT brothers aiming to live a California dream they all imagined back in Cambridge as "billionaires, bottles, and babes." With girlfriends in tow, Smith and Houston gulped glasses of Pinot and reminisced about the summer they spent coding in boxers because the A/C was down. "Those were the days," smiled Houston with his arm around Smith. "Just me and my code. None of this hiring and firing business."

Houston clearly drew strength from this group—he even recreated the fraternity living experience in San Francisco, moving into the same downtown building as Smith and ten other entrepreneurs.

If dropping out of college was a watershed moment for the likes of Bill Gates, Michael Dell, and Mark Zuckerberg, then staying in was equally transformative for Houston, particularly his fraternity experience.

The just-me-and-my-code default, after all, is wired into his DNA. His father is a Harvard-trained electrical engineer; his mother, a high school librarian. Growing up in suburban Boston, he began tinkering at age five with an IBM PC Junior. His mother, correctly deducing that her son was becoming a code geek, made him learn French and hang out with the jocks, and refused to let him skip a grade. During summers in New Hampshire she took away his computer, even as he griped about being bored in the woods. "She was subtle about making me normal, I guess, and I can appreciate it now."

At fourteen, Houston signed up to beta test an online game, and began rooting out security flaws. They soon hired him as their networking programmer, in exchange for equity. That year, at a school assembly, one speaker asked the group: "Raise your hand if you know what you want to be when you grow up." Houston was the only kid out of 250 with his hand up. "I wanted them to call on me, but it was rhetorical. I wanted to run a computer company." He worked at startups throughout high school and college. Dropbox is his sixth.

By freshman year at MIT it seemed his mom had failed. Most of his time was spent coding. He was finally convinced by Daniel Goleman's book *Emotional Intelligence* that "smarts weren't enough" if he wanted to run a company. So he spent the ensuing summer on the roof of his frat reading business books. "No one is born a CEO, but no one tells you that," says Houston. "The magazine stories make it sound like Zuckerberg woke up one day and wanted to redefine how the world communicates with a billion-dollar company. He didn't." Then he signed up to be rush and social chair, "a crash course in project management and getting people to do stuff for you." (His roommate, Joe, recalled otherwise: "No one else wanted to do it.")

When Adam Smith left the house in September 2006 to start Xobni in San Francisco, it gave Houston proper motivation. "If he could do it, I knew I could," said Houston. "I wanted to live the dream and felt stuck eating Hot Pockets." His MBA from Phi Delta Theta was complete.

The idea for Dropbox was born three months later on a bus to New York. He had planned to work during the four-hour ride from Boston but forgot his USB memory stick, leaving him with a laptop and no code to mess with. Frustrated, he immediately started building technology to synch files over the Web. Four months later he flew to San Francisco to pitch his idea to Paul Graham of incubator Y Combinator.

But Graham insisted he have a cofounder before even submitting his application. Houston had two weeks to find the right person. A friend referred him to Ferdowsi, the only son of Iranian refugees, who was studying computer science at MIT. They talked for two hours back in Boston and "got married on the second date," as Houston describes it. Ferdowsi dropped out of school with just six months to go.

Dropbox landed $15,000 from Y Combinator, enough to rent an apartment and buy a Mac. Keen to make Dropbox work on every computer, he spent twenty hours a day trying to reverse-engineer the guts of it.

Dropbox answered a new, vexing problem for a world where people carry a phone or two, and perhaps a tablet, but have files and photos stuck on multiple PCs, laptops, and mobiles. "Devices are getting smarter—your television, your car—and that means more data spread around," said Houston. "There needs to be a fabric that connects all these devices. That's what we do."

After one simple download of the Dropbox app someone could store any file instantly "in the cloud." Once it's there they can access that file from any other device and invite others to see it, too. An update to the file on one machine shows up on another.

Months later the duo presented Dropbox at a Y Combinator event. Immediately after, a slick-looking guy started chatting up Ferdowsi in Farsi. Pejman Nozad got his start as an investor during the dot-com era by exchanging commercial real estate for stakes in start-ups, notably PayPal. He operates out of a rug store ("I thought it was a joke," says Houston), and entertained the pair with Persian tea in the back. Within days he had Houston and Ferdowsi in front of Sequoia, the firm that backed Google and Yahoo, claiming, falsely, Dropbox was fielding multiple VC offers. "Basically he was our pimp," said Houston.

Sequoia's senior partner, Michael Moritz, showed up at Houston and Ferdowsi's apartment the following Saturday morning. "They were bleary-eyed," recalled Moritz. Pizza boxes climbed the walls and blankets cluttered the corners. He told his partners to do the deal, and Dropbox landed $1.2 million. "I've seen a variety of companies attacking parts of his problem, like Plaxo," said Moritz. "Big companies would go after this, I knew. I was betting they have the intellect and stamina to beat everyone else."

Houston and Ferdowsi spent the next year pulling all-nighters. They were perfectionists. One time Houston had to track down a copy of Windows XP for Sweden because it had a unique coding quirk that was stalling Dropbox slightly. Ferdowsi had a designer spend hours tweaking the shade of Dropbox's button inside the file system on a Mac. It was a touch darker than the Apple buttons, and it drove him "crazy" for weeks. "I am the gatekeeper here," said Ferdowsi. "Everything has to be just so."

Dropbox stayed lean, which enabled it to sail through the meltdown. In 2008 it had nine employees and 200,000 customers. Two and a half years later it had added five workers. Users rose tenfold.

Houston and Ferdowsi moved offices again and often just slept at work. They were getting every customer service e-mail and ignoring messages from their VCs. They toyed with advertising. "That's what you're supposed to do: hire a marketing guy, buy Google AdWords," said Houston. "We sucked at it." It was costing them $300 to hook one sign-up. Their challenge was marketing a product to solve a problem people didn't realize they had and weren't searching for. Ferdowsi from the start insisted Dropbox's home page be a simple stick-figure video showing what the product does. No table of features and pricing; instead, a story about a guy who loses stuff and goes on a trip to Africa.

So rather than advertise, they turned their small but loyal customer base into salespeople, giving away 250 megabytes of free storage in exchange for a referral. One-quarter of all new customers come to Dropbox this way. Within two and a half years the snowball had rolled into a $4 billion valuation.

The opportunity in front of Drew Houston revealed itself again in the summer of 2011 during a booze-fueled lunch at VC Ron Conway's Belvedere, California bayside villa. As Houston carefully explained what Dropbox did, he was cut off exactly as he had been by Steve Jobs so many years ago: "I know, I use it all the time." Rather than a tech CEO, his drinking buddy was rapper Will.i.am of the

Black Eyed Peas, who told Houston he used Dropbox to collaborate with producer David Guetta on the hit "I Gotta Feeling."

Such tipping-point anecdotes now pour in. After his laptop crashed during final exams, one law student wrote in: "Without Dropbox I would have failed out of law school and be living under a bridge." A watch design firm just outside of Venice, Italian Soul, used Dropbox to create new pieces with a designer in Mendoza, Argentina, the hulking 3-D files living painlessly in the cloud. Haitian relief workers kept up-to-date records of the deceased and shared those names with Miami and other cities. Professional sports teams inventory videos of opponents' plays, accessible wherever the team is playing. On Thanksgiving 2010, the shadowy Ferdowsi, donning a Dropbox hoodie, was mobbed by starstruck teens in an arcade in Kansas City, his hometown. "That's when I knew we'd hit it," said Ferdowsi.

HOUSTON BELIEVES DROPBOX IS ushering in a new wave of computing, where people are untethered from their files. "Your data follows you."

To pull this off Dropbox must manage incredible volume and stunning complexity—while making that all simply disappear to anyone using the service. As we talked with him in late 2011, 325 million files were saved daily to Dropbox (old files and newly created ones), which had to slide seamlessly onto any device. By early 2013, that number passed one billion. Houston and his geeks built tendrils into eighteen different operating systems, four browsers, and three mobile software systems. When even the smallest software update comes out, they have to make sure Dropbox still works. In June

2011 a password breach exposed up to sixty-eight accounts, underscoring the risk Houston faces as the company holding the keys to 50 million people's digital attic. "I cannot express how deeply sorry I am," he e-mailed the exposed users, appending his personal cell phone number. "Dropbox is my life."

There's also the issue of competition. Houston rattled off the list: "Apple, Google, Microsoft, Amazon in a way, then there's IDrive, YouSendIt, Box.net, dozens of startups, even e-mail . . . people sending themselves everything." While he believes Dropbox will torpedo the backup industry within five years, he especially fears iCloud, which has pushed itself upon the hundreds of millions of people who've bought iPhones, iPods, iPads, and Google's Drive product. But Apple has proved less monolithic since the passing of Houston's hero, Steve Jobs; Dropbox remains the leader.

Houston combatted an implosion by spending a lot of his war chest on ubiquity. He protected his flank against Google via a deal with phone maker HTC, which makes Dropbox the default cloud storage option on every one of its Android phones. Deals with other phone firms, plus PC and television makers came next. Houston hired a team to tailor Dropbox to businesses. Hundreds of outside developers are making apps for Dropbox.

Houston needed to delegate more. His spiky chestnut hair boasted patches of premature gray. The Phi Delta MBA remained the company's CFO until April 2014. Relinquishing that post was a big step on the road from startup code geek to tech tycoon.

A glimpse at his future came one evening in the fall of 2011. Houston dined with Mark Zuckerberg, and over generous portions of buffalo meat (the Facebook founder was then in his much-mocked phase of eating only what he killed), they plotted ways to collaborate.

As he walked out of Zuckerberg's pre-IPO starter home, a relatively modest Palo Alto colonial, clearly en route to becoming the big company CEO he had told Steve Jobs he would be, Houston noticed the security guard parked outside, presumably all day, every day, and pondered the corollaries of the path: "I'm not sure I want to live that life."

CHAPTER 3

Elon Musk, Tesla Motors and SpaceX: Inside the Mind of Iron Man

Elon Musk may be the greatest entrepreneur of the twenty-first century. By thirty-two, he had cofounded and sold two wildly successful companies, including PayPal, the bank of the Internet, which eBay bought for $1.5 billion in 2002. For a second act, he again went double-barreled, this time aiming for two of the world's largest, most hidebound industries: automobiles and space travel. With Tesla Motors, he sought to make a viable electric car (and create the first successful American auto startup in more than a half-century). SpaceX was designed to privatize the path to the heavens. Today, both seem likely winners, swelling Musk's net worth well past $10 billion.

But when **Hannah Elliott** spent extensive time with Musk in 2011 and 2012, those successes were far from certain, and his second marriage was crumbling. For months, on both coasts, Musk, now forty-three, gave Elliott full access to his work and home life, sharing his uninhibited thoughts in real time—less Tony Stark (Musk was the inspiration for Iron Man) than Tony Soprano. Not even genius, it turns out, is free from doubt.

On a Thursday morning in Bel Air, California, Elon Musk, his cheeks still wet with aftershave, retreated to the basement theater of his 20,000-square-foot French Nouveau mansion, which he's converted into a man cave suitable for business or play.

The leather couch and coffee table inscribed with the periodic table served as a de facto workstation, a retreat for the e-mails he shoots out past midnight and his research on such things as the Phenolic Impregnated Carbon Ablator, the "best heat shield known to man." But rather than trudge to the office when the rest of the world is awake, the young billionaire founder of electric car maker Tesla and SpaceX, the first private company to put a vehicle into orbit, taught me how to play BioShock, an Ayn Rand–esque first-person shooter epic.

"It talks about Hegelian dialectics being the things that determine the course of history," Musk explained, his eyes fixed on the screen. "They're sort of competing philosophies or competing meme sets, and you can look at modern history where it's not so much genetics going into battle as a battle of meme structures."

Yes, he talks like that. While he's playing video games.

The games went on for ninety minutes. While work for both of his companies beckoned—Tesla was readying the debut of an SUV aimed at eco-conscious soccer moms and planned to launch a new sedan; SpaceX, meanwhile, was testing its Dragon spacecraft for a docking with the International Space Station—Musk clearly relished the distraction, carving out still more time for a tour of the house.

Situated atop a hidden hill that overlooks the Pacific Ocean, the 1.6-acre grounds boast a tennis court (Musk's brother, Kimbal, joked that their infrequent matches get so competitive that he needs to run away after making a winning shot), an outdoor pool, and a footpath leading to a giant tree upon which Musk, the father of then-seven-year-old twins and five-year-old triplets, all boys, planned to build a tree fort. The inside was just as grand, with all the expected billionaire trappings, down to the cavernous wine cellar and the master bathroom so big Musk put a treadmill in it.

What was missing from all of this, though, was any sign of actual people. The white shelves in a towering library stood embarrassingly bare. (Musk devours books exclusively on his iPhone, including *The Autobiography of Benjamin Franklin* and Walter Isaacson's *Steve Jobs.*)

The pool was covered, the manicured backyard devoid of toys, lawn chairs, or a grill. The boys were at school—Musk, having been through a much-publicized divorce, shared custody of his sons with his college sweetheart, Justine. His second wife, Talulah Riley, a twenty-eight-year-old British actress, was, I was told, back in her home country filming a movie. There was no evidence—clothes, shoes, makeup—of a female inhabitant. There weren't even any personal photographs to speak of, save a three-foot-wide panoramic shot of Musk and Riley watching an eclipse in front of a private yacht on some remote tropical beach, his arms wrapped around her as they both gaze skyward, laughing. On another wall, a photo of a chair seemed to be the placeholder that came with the frame.

I asked Musk if he had a dog. Yes, he said, two. But no dish, leashes, or chew toys were in sight. The house, he told me, is leased. So was the furniture. Although Musk lived here, in other words, it would be an exaggeration to call it his home. It was a way station, the perfect place to play dystopian video games.

AT SIX FOOT ONE, with broad shoulders and legs that match his first name (Elon is Hebrew for "oak tree," although Musk's family comes from Pennsylvania Dutch stock, not Jewish), he filled out the burgundy Tesla Roadster—which he chose over his Audi Q7 and Porsche 911—for the twenty-mile drive to the Hawthorne-based headquarters of SpaceX. Pulling onto the 405, he attentively configured the optimum temperature and wind levels for the convertible; programmed a mix of Robbie Williams, Adele, and Beethoven's Fifth; and drove fast and clinically. It was all done in a manner that reflects his public perception as a robotic genius—the real-life inspiration for the Tony Stark character in Jon Favreau's *Iron Man*. Much of that reputation is deserved.

"If I was walking with the three kids and Elon disappeared, he was in a bookstore," recalled his mother, Maye, who, at 63, remains an in-demand fashion model. (While in her sixties, she posed in the buff with a fake baby bump, Demi Moore–style, for the cover of *New York* magazine.) "He'd be sitting on the ground in a world of his own. He read the entire *Encyclopedia Britannica* when he was only eight or nine—and he remembered it!"

Growing up in Pretoria, South Africa, Elon alienated schoolmates by correcting their minor factual errors. He thought he was doing them a favor; they thought he was arrogant and responded by bullying him.

"He can be brutally honest, where you're like, Oh my God, that stuff hurts," said his sister, Tosca. "He's not trying to be mean or make you feel bad. And he appreciates honesty in return."

By college—Musk studied physics and business at the University of Pennsylvania, then more physics and science at Stanford—he had matured physically but retained his blunt intensity, channeling it into his studies to the point where Maye felt the need to check on him to make sure he was at least getting something to eat and wore a fresh pair of socks every day. He has "become a better man" since college, said his Penn roommate Adeo Ressi, another tech entrepreneur. "Now he will make jokes."

As he drove to work—his Montblanc aviators, retrieved from the floor of the Lotus-bodied coupe, perched on his nose—we talked about his favorite drives (he favors Highway 1, unsurprisingly), his favorite music (when not rocking to Robbie Williams, he's more a Beatles and Pink Floyd, classic rock man), and his favorite cars (the 1967 Jag E-Type is "like a bad girlfriend—very dysfunctional").

"Do you ever wish you had lived during a different time in history?" I asked.

"No, I'm glad I live now," he responded, displaying the remnants of his South African lilt.

"Why?"

"If anyone thinks they'd rather be in a different part of history, they're probably not a very good student of history. Life sucked in the old days. People knew very little, and you were likely to die at a young age of some horrible disease. You'd probably have no teeth by now. It would be particularly awful if you were a woman."

Good point.

"If you go back a few hundred years, what we take for granted today would seem like magic—being able to talk to people over long distances, to transmit images, flying, accessing vast amounts of data like an oracle. These are all things that would have been considered magic a few hundred years ago. So engineering is, for all intents and purposes, magic, and who wouldn't want to be a magician?"

Musk has been one of his generation's foremost magicians almost since leaving Stanford. In 1995, he cofounded Zip2 Corporation, a software and services provider to the media industry, which he sold to Compaq in 1999 for $307 million in cash.

Then, in 1998, he cofounded PayPal, which went public in early 2002; Musk was the largest shareholder of the company until eBay acquired it for $1.5 billion later that year. His fame grew with his success—when he and Riley married in 2010, Larry Page and Sergey Brin reportedly loaned them the Google jet for their honeymoon; Musk and Riley became frequent guests at Hollywood A-list parties and chic weekend retreats.

Over the past decade, he has doubled his magic, at once trying to establish the electric car and private space industries as viable business propositions. Tesla is based in Palo Alto, so Musk commutes between the two companies twice a week via his Dassault Falcon. (Tesla's design warehouse is nearby, behind the SpaceX campus.)

Investors don't seem to mind the juggling act: Tesla went public with an IPO valued at $226.1 million. In 2011, the company posted total revenues of $204 million, with losses at $254 million. (By 2013, the revenue had surged to $2 billion, the loss whittled to $74 million.) Musk owns about 29 percent of Tesla, which has never turned a profit but, as of mid-2014, is valued at $26 billion.

Privately held SpaceX, founded in 2002 with money from the PayPal sale, has won more than $5 billion in contracts to launch satellites. In 2012, its Dragon became the first private spacecraft to shuttle to the International Space Station. In 2013, it launched a satellite into geosynchronous orbit, a feat previously pulled off only by governments. By 2014, it was successfully testing reusable rocket boosters, which could greatly shrink the cost of space flight. Pairing Dragon with its Falcon launch vehicle, Musk thinks he could have his first crewed mission by 2015.

Thirty minutes into the drive, we arrived at SpaceX, which, if you didn't know better, would seem like a movie set, right down to the life-size statue of Tony Stark in his Iron Man suit and an ice cream stand, where middle-aged engineers line up to pile toppings on their free soft-serve sundaes. The walls here are more impressively adorned than in Musk's rental house: He pointed out a portrait of Wernher von Braun, the ex-Nazi who advocated for NASA's Apollo program, and drew me over to a huge photo of Mars, a place he dreams of colonizing, and navigates me to the Valles Marineris trench. The real show, though, took place on the manufacturing floor, where the conical Dragon spacecraft awaited its date with the space station.

Surrounded by the best toys in the history of the planet, Musk returned to his office—a jumbo corner cube, actually, since SpaceX and Tesla embrace the open-seating philosophy—and grabbed a sword, its handle swathed in stingray leather, an award for accomplishments in commercial space, whisking it around his shoulders. "You could really stab somebody with this thing," he said. "I'm trying to make it swoosh without killing anyone."

I held up a sheet of paper for target practice, and Musk, true to his promise, avoided killing me, though he failed to slice the paper, instead pushing it out of my hands. He took revenge on a nearby potted plant, slicing a few leaves off with the precision of a master engineer.

AS MUCH AS ELON Musk is known for rational brilliance, he also carries a playboy reputation—nights spent dancing in Afro wigs and leisure suits, closing down Russian clubs in New York, and grokking Burning Man in full. Young, handsome, self-made, he has all the game he needs at any club, including the one in London where he met Talulah Riley, twenty-three at the time, in 2008. So it wasn't too surprising that, at midnight on a Friday in Hollywood, I was still waiting for Musk to text me.

The idea was that he would show me, with a group of his friends, *his* Los Angeles—how the City of Angels plays out when money and access are unlimited. We exchanged messages all day about it. But per his last update, he was eating a quiet dinner at Soho House with his close friend, *Iron Man* director Jon Favreau. "We can meet for a drink at the Beverly Hills Hotel (or somewhere else) afterwards," he texted.

By 12:30 a.m., though, he wasn't feeling it: "Just left Soho House. Am on way home and pretty tired. Was up early with the kids, so not much sleep." Then another message: "The reality is that I very rarely go out to clubs these days. Only did that twice in the past twelve months, because friends dragged me there." I'd been waiting with friends a few miles away at the Spare Room. Someone in my group suggested I had gotten "hot-chicked"—current L.A. lingo for being replaced by a better offer—but that didn't ring true. Later, by chance, I heard from someone who had seen Musk with Favreau at

Soho House, as he had said. And over the previous three months, he had faithfully returned every phone call, e-mail, and text I sent.

He did go dark on me once. For three weeks, through Christmas and New Year's, there had been complete silence, except to cancel a photo shoot. It was as if he had retreated into the rented man cave for extended hibernation.

A late-night tweet posted on January 17, 2013 explained everything: "@rileytalulah It was an amazing four years. I will love you forever. You will make someone very happy one day."

I e-mailed him as soon as I saw the breakup announcement—Musk, back from the breach, called me ten minutes later, at 7:00 a.m. his time. "It just became emotionally difficult," he said quietly. He sounded different: sad, yes, but also raw and alive. "Essentially, I fell out of love, and it's kind of hard to get back." It was a relief to have made the news public, he said, as it had become increasingly evident over the past few months that he and Riley weren't going to make it.

It turns out that Riley hadn't been with Musk in Los Angeles for months. According to court documents, she was the one who filed for divorce.

The second split (settled for a reported $4 million, followed almost two years later by comments that seemed to imply they have reconciled their relationship, if not their marriage) went easier than the first—a public, very acrimonious breakup in 2008 that capped what Musk has called the most difficult year of his life. Justine Musk, who did not respond to interview requests for this story, chronicled their troubles in *Marie Claire*: "The same qualities that helped bring about his extraordinary success dictate that the life you lead with him is his life . . . and that there is no middle ground (not least because he has no time to find it)." Elon Musk largely stayed mum.

Did he still believe in love? "Yeah, absolutely." Although he wasn't sure at the moment how, or where, to find it. His wish list—selfless, hardworking, realistic—didn't seem to jibe well with his old Hollywood-club ways.

MUSK'S TWO WORLDS—HOLLYWOOD AND Silicon Valley—converged when he hosted the launch party for his new Tesla SUV at the company's Hawthorne design warehouse. Musk recruited Foster the People as entertainment (three nights later, they would play the Grammys), as nearly 2,000 people, from fashionistas to venture capitalists, *Captain America* star Chris Evans to California governor Jerry Brown, washed down lobster with Veuve Clicquot and clamored for a piece of Musk.

Taking the stage in a midnight-blue velour blazer and dark jeans, Musk actually told a joke, albeit a lame one about fracking ("The world desperately needs sustainable transport. If we don't solve this problem this century, we are fracked!") and stood calmly watching as designers frantically tried to open the overstuffed front trunk of the SUV. ("We're maybe a bit stuck on the safety latch there," he said.) He stayed late, appeared to drink only water, and posed gamely with the many women around him asking for photos—without seeming to focus on anyone in particular. Half the time he sat on a couch in a corner surrounded by well-groomed men wearing sports jackets and loafers.

The night was crucial for Musk, who touted the "falcon wing" SUV as the ideal combination of a minivan (practicality), Audi Q7 (style), and Porsche 911 (performance)—and the logical follow-up to his $50,000 Model S electric sedan, which debuted in 2012. He needed a hit: In 2012, Tesla boasted a $3.6 billion market cap but sold only 2,000 or so of the discontinued Roadsters.

Yet he seemed as relaxed as I've seen him. There was a waiting list for both the SUV and the upcoming sedan, and he was wearing the clarity of his personal life with ease. Two days later, I came back for another morning at his mansion, and this time, the house was jumping. It was Saturday, so the kids were off from school—Dad and the boys loudly played a variant of dodgeball they called "dog-ball." (He and his old roommate Ressi started taking their kids on Daddy camping trips in Yosemite.)

Meanwhile, I was with a large photography crew, including three photo assistants, a makeup artist, and a fashion director, plus a blonde Frenchwoman sent to mind the $35,090 Parmigiani wrist-watch Musk would wear for the photos. Musk, unexpectedly, rolled with it. At a previous shoot earlier that week, he had vetoed imme-diately the tailored offerings from Tom Ford, Giorgio Armani, and Ralph Lauren set out for him. "You'll have to find something else," he had announced to the stylist. "I will not look like some preppy boy. That's not me."

He wound up warming to the selections and even bought a few items on the spot. And he happily donned what had been requested, whistling Sinatra as he changed.

On my way to the airport, I thanked him via e-mail for his hos-pitality and for introducing us all to his children. His quick response was typically to the point: "You're welcome. Things are good with business and kids. Just need to figure out the romantic side (or be-come a monk)."

CHAPTER 4

Kevin Systrom, Instagram: No Revenues? No Revenue Model? No Problem!

What does $1 billion look like in this new era? Fourteen twentysomethings—the entirety of Instagram's head count—banging away on keyboards in the company's small office in San Francisco's SoMa neighborhood. How fast does it take to get to $1 billion? In this case, twenty-two months, from idea to exit. And what kind of financial metrics equate to $1 billion? For Instagram, there were none. No revenue, no expressed way to get any. These kind of facts led many to conclude that Facebook's $1 billion purchase, in 2012, was a sure sign of a bubble. In reality, it was one of the great deals of the Internet age—by 2014, the company was likely worth $10 billion. Instagram—and its 200 million active users, who share 60 million photos a day—offered a seamless path onto mobile phones.

When **Steven Bertoni** sat down with founder Kevin Systrom, now thirty, for his first-ever in-depth profile, Instagram

was in limbo. The deal was done, yet the check hadn't arrived and Facebook corporate minders were nowhere to be
found. Systrom was in limbo, too. He knew he was about to
be incredibly wealthy, but he was still living on a bootstrap
budget. Perhaps outside the money, little has changed since:
Systrom remains at the helm of the company—which operates independently from Facebook's Menlo Park campus—
his lean team of coders trying to scale, hopeful that the app
can become the eyes of the world.

———

Kevin Systrom was working behind a hissing espresso machine at
Palo Alto's Caffè del Doge in the spring of 2006 when Facebook
founder Mark Zuckerberg approached the counter with a puzzled
look on his face. The previous summer Zuckerberg had taken Systrom to dinner at Zao Noodle Bar on University Avenue and asked
him to ditch his senior year at Stanford to develop a photo service for
his nascent social network, The Facebook. Systrom turned down the
offer. Now Facebook, sans the "The," was worth $500 million—en
route to a valuation more than 300 times greater—and making
headlines. Systrom was making cappuccinos.

"I had been like, 'No, I don't want to work at this thing,' and here I
am working at a cafe,'" Systrom, then twenty-eight, told me over our
$4.50 cups of artisanal coffee in the warehouse-like room of Sightglass
Coffee in San Francisco's SoMa district. By opting to stay at Stanford he
had turned down what surely would have amounted to tens of millions
in Facebook options. "Working at a startup to make a lot of money was
never a thing, and that's why I decided to just finish up school. That

was way more important for me," shrugged Systrom. "I'm sure in retrospect it would have been a nice deal, but it's funny where you end up."

In Systrom's case, the place you end up is exactly the place you turned down—Facebook. But thanks to his Stanford detour, instead of eight figures, Systrom, by doing it his own way—developing the white-hot photo network Instagram, which Zuckerberg agreed to buy in 2012—now stood atop a $1 billion score. The purchase price, which made Systrom's stake of 40 percent or so worth $400 million, is all the more shocking given that his startup had zero revenues and no revenue model. Instagram, just twenty-two months old, still had all of fourteen employees.

But what Systrom also had—and which Facebook, at the time reeling after a choppy public debut, desperately needed—was buzz, and a mobile platform that had prompted more than eighty-five million users to share four billion photos, with six new members joining every second.

"This is the first thing I've seen that feels like it's truly native to mobile," said Matt Cohler, the former VP of product management at Facebook and current general partner with Instagram investor Benchmark Capital. "To have scaled the product, the network of users, and the infrastructure behind it, is nothing short of extraordinary under any circumstance; to do it with such a small team is unique in the annals of technology."

While the Web-based biggies tried to jam their products into mobile apps like an overstuffed suitcase into an overhead bin, Instagram's photo network was jet-set from the start: fast, stylish, and elegant. With a few simple thumb taps you could snap, edit (with awesome filters), and share an Instagram photo with the world. A few more taps let you do all the things that built Facebook, including comments and likes. "You can look at Facebook as this bundle of so many different things, but it turns out that people just like photos more than anything else," said Adam D'Angelo, the former Facebook CTO who took over the question site Quora and invested early in Instagram. "So if you specialize in photos and do photos really well, that's in some way more powerful than this bundle of everything else."

Systrom offered early proof that in the digital economy a great idea can grow into a billion-dollar company in a matter of months. But these windfalls, serendipitous as they seem from the outside, are almost never accidental. In Systrom's case, his good fortune can be traced directly to Stanford.

The Palo Alto campus provided Systrom his first look at the worlds of tech and venture capital, his first internship at a startup, and his first job at Google. He discovered his love for vintage photography through a Stanford study-abroad program and met Zuckerberg and his young Facebook crew at a Stanford fraternity party. When he was searching for a cofounder to launch the company that later morphed into Instagram, it was a Stanford connection that brought the pair together. "When people say that college isn't worthwhile and paying all this money isn't worthwhile, I really disagree," said Systrom. "I think those experiences and those classes that may not necessarily seem applicable in the moment end up coming back to you time and time again."

SYSTROM, A LANKY SIX foot five, loved technology well before his college years. At age twelve he was pranking his friends in Holliston, Massachusetts over AOL with programs that allowed him to control their cursors or knock them offline (his Bart Simpson antics got the family AOL account blocked). He applied early to Stanford, with the intent of studying computer science, but after enrolling in an advanced programming course in his freshman year, Systrom found himself over his head, spending forty hours a week on one class just to squeak out a B: "I loved it but started to think maybe I shouldn't be a computer scientist." Instead, he majored in management science and engineering. "It basically taught me how to be an investment banker."

Long interested in entrepreneurship and startups (his mom was an early employee of Monster.com and then worked at Zipcar), Systrom spent his free time building websites, such as a Stanford version of Craigslist. Another site, which he called Photobox, was a place for his fraternity, Sigma Nu, to post photos from the latest keg party.

During junior year Systrom traveled abroad to study photography in Florence, Italy. He arrived in Italy with a high-powered SLR camera only to see his photo teacher swap it for a Holga camera. The cheap plastic device produced quirky square images with soft focus and light distortions that yielded a retro look. Systrom loved the aesthetic. "It taught me the beauty of vintage photography and also the beauty of imperfection." It was Systrom's Steve Jobs moment—a flash of artistic inspiration that he would later combine with technology to rocket Instagram ahead of its competitors.

While in Florence, Systrom applied to Stanford's elite Mayfield Fellows Program: a work-study seminar that threw twelve students into the world of startups and paired them with entrepreneur and VC mentors. "It taught you fundraising, how deals were structured, how they came up with ideas and hired people. It was a crash-course business school for startups," Systrom said. The program's codirector, Tina Seelig, said Systrom stood out as an obvious entrepreneur: "He was always building things—always experimenting. It was in his nature to be looking at the world through the lens of 'Where's the opportunity here?'"

Through the Mayfield program, Systrom snagged a summer internship at Odeo, a podcast company founded by Evan Williams that would later birth Twitter. Odeo gave Systrom his first taste of the adrenaline-filled startup environment and showed him how quick, flexible thinking was vital to a company's survival. During his internship Systrom created apps with a young engineer named Jack Dorsey, who would soon start Twitter and the payment company Square. It was a key connection: The two nonvegans in the office quickly bonded on runs for deli sandwiches, and Dorsey would later help Instagram get off the ground, building demand for its filtered photos by posting images on his much-followed Twitter account.

Senior year, with help from Stanford career services, Systrom passed on a six-figure project manager role at Microsoft to stay local with a Google marketing gig that paid about $60,000. Google was a recent graduate's dream—oyster lunches, team-building retreats in Brazil—but Systrom grew bored writing marketing copy for Gmail and Google Calendar. Denied a role in product development (Google required a computer science degree) he switched to corporate development, where he modeled discounted cash flows for companies Google aimed to acquire and saw firsthand how big technology deals got done.

Hungry for the startup environment he found while interning with Odeo, Systrom jumped to a social travel guide site called Nextstop, where he turned himself into a Valley-grade coder, designing e-mail programs that suggested users to follow and building Face-book photo games. "All of a sudden I had a new skill that I could actually put to use," says Systrom. "When you had an idea you could actually create it."

Soon he found something he wanted to create: a site that would combine his passion for photos with location check-ins and social gaming, mimicking the then-surging Foursquare and Zynga, respectively. He chatted up his idea—then known as Burbn, after his favorite booze—at a VC meet-up at the Madrone Art Bar and caught the ear of Baseline Ventures' Steve Anderson. Anderson says he liked Systrom's humble confidence and that Systrom's site would be written in the then "it" code of HTML5. In the winter of 2010, Anderson offered him $250,000 to launch the company (and venture capital firm Andreessen Horowitz matched that stake) on one condition—Systrom needed to bring in a cofounder.

SYSTROM'S STANFORD DIVIDENDS CONTINUED long after graduation. He launched Burbn in the living room of his one-bedroom San Francisco apartment and would often work on the prototype at Coffee Bar in the Mission so that he could see other humans. There he'd sometimes bump into Mike Krieger, a Brazilian native who had graduated from Stanford's Mayfield program two years behind Systrom and was working on apps of his own. Krieger had majored in symbolic systems—a Stanford mash-up of technology and psychology that counts LinkedIn's Reid Hoffman and Yahoo's Marissa Mayer as alumni—and was working at a chat site, Meebo. On one occasion, Systrom let Krieger download his new check-in app. "I wasn't superenthusiastic about location-based things, but Burbn was the first one that I loved," Krieger told me, noting it was the ability to view photos of his friends' various adventures that had him hooked.

A month later Systrom invited Krieger to breakfast to convince him to quit Meebo and join Burbn as a cofounder. Krieger's response: "Count me interested; we'll talk more." The pair field-tested the partnership—working on small programs after work and over weekends—and after a few weeks Systrom proved more persuasive than Zuckerberg had been years earlier. Krieger quit Meebo and started what would be a three-month process to obtain a U.S. work visa.

On Krieger's first day on the job, though, Systrom declared that Burbn wouldn't survive—Foursquare had too much traction. They had to build something new and decided to streamline Burbn into a photo-only, mobile-focused service. "The iPhone was so new, and people were creating really cool stuff and creating new behaviors," Systrom said. "It was an opportunity to create a new type of service, a social network that wasn't based on a computer but the computer in your hand."

Over the course of two weeks the cofounders hunkered down at Dogpatch Labs near AT&T Park, cranking out a photo app they called Codename. Krieger designed the Apple iOS software while Systrom worked on the back-end code. The prototype was basically an iPhone camera app with social and commenting functions. Neither was too excited about what they had built. Frustrated, Systrom needed a break.

He rented a cheap house at an artist colony in Baja California, Mexico for a week's vacation. While walking down the beach, his girlfriend, Nicole Schuetz, asked how one of their friends posted such amazing-looking photos over the app. His answer? Filters. Suddenly Systrom remembered his experience with the cheap camera in Florence. He spent the rest of the day lying on a hammock, a bottle of Modelo beer sweating by his side, as he typed away at his laptop researching and designing the first Instagram filter that would become X-Pro II.

Back in San Francisco, new filters soon followed, like Hefe (named after the hefeweizen beer Systrom drank while designing it) and Toaster (in honor of the labradoodle owned by Digg founder Kevin Rose). They renamed the product Instagram and gave the new app to friends—many of them tech influencers like Twitter's Dorsey—who started posting their filtered photos to social networks. Buzz began to build.

Instagram gives low-quality camera phone pics a hip, retro feel. One tap on the touchscreen and an average sunset changes into a tropical postcard, an old bicycle gets a sting of nostalgia, and a half-eaten hamburger turns poignant. "Imagine if there was a funny button in Twitter or a clever button in Tumblr," said Systrom. "Most photo apps before asked something of the users. They said, You produce, act, and perform. Instagram said, Let us take care of the secret sauce."

Recipe in hand, Systrom and Krieger launched Instagram on the Apple app store at midnight on October 6, 2010. Users flowed in, and Systrom and Krieger rushed to Dogpatch Labs to keep the servers stable. By 6:00 a.m. media sites like Bits Blog and TechCrunch had published stories about the debut. The servers melted. Systrom and Krieger worked a straight twenty-four hours to keep the app running—in that period 25,000 iPhone users downloaded the free service.

"From that day on we never had the same life," said Systrom. They called on Quora's Adam D'Angelo, whom Systrom had met with Zuckerberg at a Stanford frat party, who helped Instagram get on Amazon.com servers and scale the platform. After one month, Instagram had a million users. Soon Systrom found himself sitting in the fourth row at Apple's keynote watching Steve Jobs highlight the app before the crowd. They had made it to technology's biggest stage, but keeping the Instagram servers running as users joined by the millions was still proving to be a major challenge.

AS WE HUNG OUT in a booth at a cocktail bar called Tradition—Systrom, Krieger, and two early employees, Josh Riedel and Shayne Sweeney—it was easy to forget that these four twentysomethings in indigo jeans and untucked button-downs were running a billion-dollar tech company. But when Krieger noticed that a photo he snapped of the bar menu had yet to receive any likes (with 177,000 followers, the response was usually instantaneous), a MacBook Air, a Verizon Hotspot, and a pile of iPhones materialized among the glasses of cask-finished bourbon.

Krieger dug through code on his laptop as the others texted with Instagram engineers via Facebook chat. They found the glitch and went to work. A few minutes later the problem was solved, the gadgets were tucked away, and another round was ordered. "It's our baby," said Systrom. "It keeps us up at night and wakes us up in the morning." Company policy requires engineers to keep a laptop on them at all times. Computers have been whipped out during birthday parties, date nights, and wedding receptions. Once, Krieger was dining at a farm-to-table restaurant when the system crashed. He frantically roamed the grounds for a wireless connection until he finally found one bar of service—inside a chicken coop.

These feats of server acrobatics ended once the Facebook deal was finalized in September 2012. The growing team could tap into Zuckerberg's massive network infrastructure. The deal, Systrom said, happened during a frenzied week in April after he returned from a UK vacation. That Wednesday Instagram was wired $50 million in a series B round from venture capitalists including Greylock, Sequoia, and Thrive Capital, valuing the company at $500 million. On Saturday Zuckerberg invited Systrom to his Palo Alto home. This time Systrom took Zuck's offer. By Monday the billion-dollar deal—including $300 million in cash—was done.

Facebook's purchase of Instagram—a company that, at the time of the purchase, had yet to earn a dollar—caused many in the media to scream, "Bubble!" Meanwhile, some insiders were whispering, "Bargain!" "It was worth much more than that. I think Facebook got a great deal," said Quora's D'Angelo. "It was probably very scary to Facebook that someone else might own Instagram or that it might turn into its own social network. . . . The fact is that everyone is coordinated on this one thing to share photos, and you can't move them all out onto something else. The network has been built out. It's too late."

With the benefit of time, it now appears that Facebook did get a bargain. Instagram, today with 200 million active users, was a cheap way for Zuckerberg to jump into the mobile game. In fact many barstool philosophers around the Valley—prompted by Facebook's failed $3 billion acquisition of Snapchat and successful bids for WhatsApp ($19 billion) and Oculus VR ($2 billion)—theorize that, as of 2014, an independent Instagram would have been worth $10 billion. We'll never know.

What is certain: Systrom is now both very wealthy and still in charge of the company he cofounded. Unlike his other acquisitions, which are quickly absorbed into Facebook, Zuckerberg publicly pledged to let Systrom run Instagram independently. Systrom and Krieger now use Facebook's muscle to scale and shape Instagram into a more substantial service. Their goal: transforming Instagram from a photo app for sharing pics of puppies and pizza into a media company that communicates through photos.

"Imagine the power of surfacing what's happening in the world through images, and potentially other types of media in the future, to each and every person who holds a mobile phone," Systrom told me. At its best Instagram would be a pocket-size window to the world that would deliver a live view of what's unfolding across the globe—say, Syrian street protests or the Super Bowl sidelines. "I think they have a Thomas Edison–like opportunity," says Thrive Capital's Joshua Kushner. "At some point . . . you'll go onto Instagram and see what's happening in real time anywhere in the world, and that's world-changing."

Then there's the whole revenue thing. Facebook does not break down Instagram revenue, but the platform has won large marketing campaigns from the likes of Heineken, Mercedes-Benz, Oreo, and Armani. Systrom predicted this back in 2012: "I think the visual format works well with advertisers. If you follow Burberry or Banana Republic, you see their Instagram posts are really ads—but they're also beautiful. Right now we're focusing on growth. It's not about squeezing a buck out of an advertiser."

He's similarly cash-oblivious at home. Systrom, who still lived in the same one-bedroom apartment, relished his relatively shoestring life. On another night I headed with the Instagram gang to the old

Army bowling alley in San Francisco's Presidio to celebrate an employee's birthday. Four Instagramers and I squeezed into Systrom's black 2002 BMW that he had bought used when he worked at Google. The car's GPS was broken, and the $400 million man almost mistakenly steered us across the Golden Gate Bridge. "I think not focusing on money makes you sane," he said. "Because in the long run it can probably drive you crazy."

CHAPTER 5

Daniel Ek, Spotify: Hacking the Music Industry

To a stunning degree, the business disruption caused by this coterie of Internet-savvy *enfants terribles* is an all-American affair. No one proves that better than Spotify's Daniel Ek, the only non-U.S. citizen to belong in the company of this book. While this shy founder, who just passed thirty, is in fact Swedish, with headquarters in Stockholm, his base of operations increasingly shifts toward New York, with his money now flowing from Silicon Valley. While many of his digital peers feel the need to destroy the old economy village in order to save it, when it comes to the songs business, Ek has a distinct advantage: Hackers had already started that job, and Steve Jobs and iTunes largely finished it. When **Steven Bertoni** began hopscotching across the Atlantic with him in the second half of 2011, Ek was regarded by many as the most important man in music, perhaps even the person wearing the white hat. By 2014, when Apple bought Spotify's largest competitor, Beats, for a staggering $3.2 billon (that number buttressed, of course, by their high-end headsets), almost 25 percent of recorded music revenues was generating via streaming.

———

On a typically damp, dark November afternoon in Stockholm, Daniel Ek was ill. Over the past month, the chief executive of Spotify, then twenty-eight, had worn himself down jetting from his Swedish base to San Francisco, New York, Denmark, the Netherlands, and France to visit his expanding sales force and launch his music service in one or another of the dozen countries in which it now operates.

But there was no rest for the weary. He'd scheduled a return to New York the following week for his first-ever press conference, to unveil Spotify's new platform. A platform that he privately admitted still wasn't ready for a public debut. "I should be home in bed," sighed Ek, his voice weak and scratchy, "but we need to get this thing perfect." So the bald, barrel-chested Ek zipped his white hoodie to his chin, swapped tea for his morning cup of coffee—the first of six he throws down in a typical day—and headed into an office that resembled a university library during finals. The pool table had been traded for more IKEA desks, and gray daybeds offered a place to nap between all-nighters. Forgoing his large office, which he mostly used as a meeting room, Ek plopped himself down at an open desk. Around him, a dozen engineers from nearly as many countries, united by their geek-chic uniforms—skinny jeans, printed T-shirts, and cardigans—frantically banged out code on their silver MacBooks.

All this frenetic energy reflected the strange new reality of the music business. More than New York or L.A. or Nashville, this rented office space along Stockholm's Birger Jarlsgatan had become the most important place in music, with Ek standing as the industry's most important player. Superstar bands like the Red Hot Chili Peppers—formed the year Ek was born—now trekked to Sweden to kiss the ring; his iPhone boasted a picture of himself cruising with Neil Young in a white 1959 Lincoln Continental; his texts were filled with breezy messages from Bono. "Both my [maternal] grandparents were in the music industry," shrugged Ek, "so I'm fairly grounded about the whole thing."

The music industry had been waiting more than a decade for Ek. Or more specifically, someone—anyone—who could build something (a) more enticing to consumers than piracy while (b) providing a sustainable revenue model. In the 1990s Shawn Fanning and Sean Parker essentially broke the recording industry with their short-lived illegal download site, Napster, which Ek describes as "the Internet experience that changed me the most." It was fast and free and limitless—through the site Ek discovered his two favorite bands, the Beatles and Led Zeppelin—and he became one of the eighteen-to-thirty-year-olds now considered a lost generation: those who don't believe you need to pay for music.

In building his iTunes juggernaut out of the wreckage, Steve Jobs subsequently proved that the cure could be almost as destructive as the disease. By training consumers to buy singles, rather than the CDs that had been the industry's lifeblood, and taking an outsize cut of the action, Apple stoked the continuing downward spiral. Recording industry revenue, a healthy $56.7 billion in 1999, according to IBISWorld, clocked in at about $30 billion in 2011.

Enter a third disrupter, Ek. In the tech landscape, where Google provided the search, Facebook the identity, and Amazon the retail, Ek wanted Spotify to supply the soundtrack. As he described it: "We're bringing music to the party." Which explains what's keeping his sleep-addled engineers on a twenty-four-hour cycle: Rather than a mere music player—albeit one with a revolutionary model that allows legal access to almost every song you've ever heard of, on demand, for free—Spotify aimed to create an entire music ecosystem.

For a consumer, Spotify is an easy sell: The service's 24 million active users (people who have listened in the past month, as of mid-2014) have access to more than 20 million songs on their desktops, all for the cost of hearing an occasional advertisement. It has the speed and ease of iTunes, the flexibility and breadth of Napster, and the attractive pricing of online radio service Pandora. And unlike those predecessors, Spotify has been social from the start, with tools that let you share playlists with pals—more than one billion songs were swapped via Facebook in its very first month on the social network.

After he was bounced as Facebook's first president, Sean Parker begged Ek to let him invest: "Ever since Napster I've dreamt of building a product similar to Spotify," his introductory e-mail read. The service impressed Mark Zuckerberg, too. "I checked it out and I thought, This is pretty amazing," the Facebook founder told me. "They internalized a lot of what we've talked about in terms of social design of apps." That means turning the core product—in Ek's case, a hard-fought song library—loose on third-party app developers to help Spotify evolve, making it even more tempting to potential customers.

Here's how that social stickiness translates into revenue: You explore your friends' playlists, discover new music with apps from Rolling Stone, Billboard, and Last.fm, and build your own jukebox. Eventually you want to take it everywhere. That's where Ek has you trapped. With Spotify you pay for portability—$10 a month buys you access to your collection on your mobile device.

According to Mark Dennis, who ran Sony Music in Sweden, Spotify single-handedly stemmed a decade of nonstop revenue drop when it launched in 2008; by 2011 Sweden's music industry saw its first growth since the Clinton Administration, with Spotify accounting for 50 percent of all sales (up from 25 percent the previous year). This in a country that was long a hotbed of piracy.

Extrapolate that on a global scale, and the music industry felt like it had its magic bullet. Roughly one-quarter of Spotify's users currently subscribe to the premium plan—that's ten million people who now lend credence to Ek's original pitch that he could rescue the record labels by waging a three-front battle with Apple, Amazon, and Google—and give their product away for free.

THE TWO FACETS OF Spotify—music and technology—were introduced to Daniel Ek at age five, when over the course of a few months he received a guitar (his mother's parents had been an opera singer and a jazz pianist) and a Commodore 20 computer (his father left the family when Ek was a baby, but his stepfather worked in IT). He was a natural at both instruments. Within two years he was writing basic code as MTV played in the background of his family apartment in the rough neighborhood of Ragsved (known to the locals as "Drugsved").

At fourteen Ek latched onto the late-1990s dot-com mania,

making commercial websites in his school's computer lab. The going rate then for a commercial home page was $50,000, but Ek charged $5,000 and made it up in volume: He recruited his teenage friends, training the math whizzes in HTML and the artists in Photoshop. Soon he was netting $15,000 a month and buying every videogame out there (one favorite: a business game called Capitalism).

True to the first generation to grow up online, he sought to master everything Internet. He bought some servers to see what made them tick, and wound up earning another $5,000 a month hosting Web pages. At sixteen, obsessed with Google's speed, he applied to be an engineer there ("Google said, 'Come back when you have a degree.'") and then set out to build his own search company.

That project failed, but led to a gig at a company called Jajja, where he worked on search engine optimization. The money was good, but the high schooler wasn't really into it. He used the paychecks to buy more servers and tuners to chase his latest obsession: recording every program on TV at once (he had no clue TiVo was pulling off the same trick). The stacks of servers in his room got so hot that Ek would strip to his underwear as soon as he walked in.

After high school Ek enrolled in Sweden's Royal Institute of Technology to study engineering. After eight weeks, realizing that the entire first year would focus solely on theoretical mathematics, he dropped out. Eventually a Stockholm-based ad network called Tradedoubler asked him to build a program to tell them about the sites they contracted with, and Ek built something so effective that the company paid him about $1 million for the rights to it in 2006; he made another $1 million selling related patents.

Then things fell apart. A self-made millionaire at twenty-three,

Ek found himself holed up alone in the woods twenty miles south of Stockholm enduring a harsh Swedish winter and a harsher bout of depression. Seeking the fast life, he had bought a three-bedroom apartment in central Stockholm, a cherry-red Ferrari Modena, and entrée to the city's hottest clubs. But it was still hard to attract girls, and the big spending attracted the wrong ones. "I was deeply uncertain of who I was and who I wanted to be," Ek said. "I really thought I wanted to be a much cooler guy than what I was."

Miserable, he sold the Ferrari and moved into a cabin near his parents, where he played guitar and meditated. Ek had already started three tech companies, but he now toyed with the idea of getting by as a professional musician. (Ek plays guitar, bass, drums, piano, and harmonica; he doesn't sing.) "I wouldn't be rich, but I could have made a living." There in the woods Ek finally decided he'd somehow marry music and tech, the two passions that drove him. During this time Ek started hanging out with Tradedoubler's chairman, Martin Lorentzon, who had fifteen years on him, but similar stamina (he works out twice a day). A Silicon Valley veteran (AltaVista), Lorentzon took Tradedoubler public in 2005, netting himself $70 million. No longer involved in the day-to-day operations, he too was bored and adrift. The first time Ek visited Lorentzon's Stockholm apartment he found only a mattress and a laptop balancing on an IKEA chair. "I asked him when he had moved in," says Ek. "When he said it had been more than a year ago, I knew he wasn't happy."

The pair bonded over marathons of gangster films like the *Godfather* trilogy and *Carlito's Way* (a ritual they repeat each year). "I got a very strong feeling when I met Daniel," said Lorentzon. "To partner up I have to like the person like a brother, because we'll face so many problems. The value of a company is the sum of the problems you solve together."

Ek doubted Lorentzon would leave Tradedoubler, so later in 2006 he set a one-week deadline. Before they committed to partnering, Lorentzon would have to publicly resign as chairman and transfer a million euros of seed money into Ek's account. The next Monday Tradedoubler sent out a press release announcing Martin Lorentzon's resignation. Later that day he told Ek to check his bank account. The money was there. The two men had yet to decide the type of business they would start.

LORENTZON AND EK WERE in a unique place: The former no longer needed the money, and the latter no longer cared about it. So they decided to ignore the dollars and aim for disruption. Their target: music. "It disturbed me that the music industry had gone down the drain, even though people were listening to more music than ever and from a greater diversity of artists," said Ek.

Sitting in two different rooms at Ek's apartment, the pair yelled out possible titles for a music site—without even yet knowing what it would do—when Ek misheard one of Lorentzon's suggestions. He typed the word "Spotify" into Google. There were zero hits (today: 23 million). Ek and Lorentzon registered the name, and started working on the ad-based plan. Once that gelled, they recruited a handful of engineers and took the new team to Barcelona to party and listen to what Ek calls "weird German electro-pop." Then they got to work.

Back in Stockholm they built a prototype based on the interface of Apple's iTunes and the sleek black styling of Ek's Samsung flat-screen TV. Unlike music sites that had launched with pirated music, Ek wouldn't debut Spotify until he signed deals with the labels. "We wanted to show that we were not in it to use their content to flip the company like others have done," Ek said.

Ek, with the help of industry lawyer Fred Davis, initially tried to get global music rights and was quickly turned down. So he aimed for European licenses, which he figured would take three months—it took two years. Ek and his team hounded label execs, pitching them that their free, ad-based model would eventually lead to more sales. No one bit. "They'd say, 'Yeah, this sounds really interesting,' or 'Send me over some stats,' which really means 'There's no way in hell we're going to do this,'" Ek said and laughed. "But I was twenty-three at the time, and I thought, Wow, this is great, we're going to get this done."

Ek eventually loaded Spotify with pirated songs and sent demos to industry execs. That got them noticed. "With Spotify people don't get it until they try it," Ek said. "Then they tell their friends." As Ek negotiated with the music companies, Spotify burned through cash. On top of salaries and overhead, Ek and Lorentzon were pledging million-dollar advances to labels for access to their music catalogs. VCs wouldn't touch them. To stay afloat they plowed nearly $5 million into Spotify, atop the $2 million Lorentzon had originally seeded. "We bet our personal fortunes, and sometimes we bet the entire company," said Ek. "We led with our conviction rather than rationale, because rationale said it was impossible." In October 2008 Spotify went live in Scandinavia, France, the U.K., and Spain. It took nearly three more years to finalize deals in the U.S.

"He's the only tech entrepreneur who's had the patience to achieve what he has with the record business," said Sean Parker, now a Spotify board member, who helped open the door to U.S. deals, including one with Facebook. "He has this Zen-like patience and an ability not to crack under pressure or get frustrated. Over and over again he puts himself in a situation where a normal person would have thrown in the towel." As I talked with Ek in his office, he sat straight and motionless like a Swedish Buddha; the only thing moving was his mouth; he wasn't even blinking his icy blue eyes.

Such calm helps him manage the chaos: In 2011 Ek was on the road 100 days—mostly a triangle between Europe, New York, and California, a schedule that cost him his girlfriend of two years. When he's in Stockholm, Ek wakes around 8:30 a.m., answers e-mail for an hour, then takes the five-minute walk to Spotify. He spends about 25 percent of his time recruiting; otherwise he's at his open desk or walking the floor. "Ek's one of the few people," said Parker, "who can handle the technology side, the strategic side, and the deal side of the business."

Ek works in the office until 8:00 p.m., eats dinner out and then returns home to unwind, either by playing guitar for a few hours or juggling a rotating trio of books (when we spoke, the Steve Jobs biography, a primer on typography, and a guide to bonzai trees). Then he hops back on e-mail, before typically turning in around 2:00 a.m. Lorentzon wants Ek to find a balance: more exercise, less junk food, more sleep, less work. The last goal will be tough to achieve for the foreseeable future.

EK BOUNDED UP ONTO the sleek white stage in Greenwich Village's Stephan Weiss Studio right after Thanksgiving in 2011, as dozens of typing journalists and rows of live TV cameras stood ready. Though thrilled that the new platform was set for launch, he couldn't wait for his first press conference to end. When Ek operated just in Europe, he could lie low. But with Spotify's entrance to America—home to the cults of Bezos, Gates, Zuckerberg, and Jobs—Ek had to switch from programmer to preacher. For Spotify to scale, he needed to hype his platform, generate buzz, and get labels, artists, and developers excited to partner up.

He didn't need to win over investors. Ek's roster had surged over the past few years. Spotify went from some smallish Swedish funding to a heavyweight round from social media elite (Li Ka-shing, Sean Parker, and Founders Fund), who collectively put in more than $50 million at a roughly $250 million valuation. A few months before the press conference, DST, Accel, and Kleiner Perkins reportedly invested close to $100 million at a $1 billion valuation. "Daniel was an entrepreneur that we had to, and wanted to, work with," said Accel's Jim Breyer. "The combination of a passion for music as well as his idea of making music as frictionless as possible for discovery and sharing is where we hit it off." Ek still held about 15 percent of the company. Thanks to all that seed money, Lorentzon owned some 20 percent. With a valuation, by the summer of 2014, swelling toward the $4 billion range, both seem poised for billion-dollar scores.

Facebook deserves a lot of credit, as well. The social media giant is embedded into Ek's platform, and vice versa. Those billions of shared songs don't happen by accident. "I don't think there's a Facebook app so well-resourced," said Ek. "We wanted it perfect." Added Zuckerberg: "He clearly is very forward-thinking on where he wants to go. He's very clear on the things he wants for the product and what he doesn't want."

The real threat to Ek, ultimately, isn't his product—it's the industry Spotify purports to save. Spotify will only be as successful as its music library. While almost every band has capitulated to the stream (the Beatles, one of Ek's favorites, still haven't played ball), others, like the Black Keys and Radiohead, have complained about the cut given to artists, despite $1 billion-plus paid in royalties to date. Scooter Braun, agent to Justin Bieber, understands the thinking but told me: "They should then tell radio not to play records for free and call YouTube and say don't allow my music to stream on videos for free."

Similarly, Ek remains vulnerable to record labels, which control all that music. Wisely, Ek brought the big players into the tent—as part of the original licensing deals, Spotify granted equity stakes to the four largest music labels (Warner, Universal, EMI, and Sony) and Merlin. Industry sources put their collective cut at nearly 20 percent. But those stakes, while significant, aren't enough to automatically quell an insurrection. Ultimately Ek needs to change the power dynamic, and create the world's dominant music source, a hit maker so big no label or artist can afford to opt out.

That's why he opened up Spotify to developers: He's hoping they'll turn it into a universal music platform, while allowing him to focus his full-time team, now 1,200 strong, solely on growth. "Google has 30,000 employees," Ek said. "A part of me wonders, What if they were all focused on really solving search?" He took out his iPhone. Using its Siri voice software, he asked it when tomorrow's first appointment begins. After a few seconds the computerized voice replied, 11:00 a.m. "Imagine if this was three times as fast or truly understood my intent," said Ek. "It's probably the biggest threat to Google; it's a whole new way of interacting."

Did he plan on building a voice-activated Spotify interface? He flashed a mischievous smile. "Play me some Coldplay," he told the phone. Its small speakers ring out with the opening piano chords of the band's hit "The Scientist." "We hacked into it a few weeks ago," Ek said, with a satisfied nod. "I'm not an inventor. I just want to make things better."

CHAPTER 6

Aaron Levie, Box:
The Man Who Would Be Gates

It's a measure of a phenomenon when an entrepreneur in his twenties raises more venture money than almost anyone in history ($414 million), yet gets privately critiqued for the "small" fortune he's left for himself ($100 million). Aaron Levie, founder of Box, clearly has a bigger prize in mind than just making himself rich—he's determined, with a stunning amount of moxie, to take on and defeat the biggest giants in tech history: IBM, Oracle, and Microsoft. If Drew Houston's Dropbox wants to be your personal digital attic, Levie's Box wants to be your office's digital file cabinets. Bill Gates and Larry Ellison, take note: As **Victoria Barret** discovered in 2013, the man fixated on some of your most lucrative business has proven himself an adept battle commander, down to his neon Pumas, with a giant IPO in his immediate field of vision.

When Aaron Levie was twenty-six, back in 2011, he did something arguably foolish, undeniably gutsy, and entirely counter to the prevailing mood that startups should be "lean" in the Internet age. Forty-five minutes into a routine meeting with his board at his simply named company, Box, Levie blithely announced: "I want to make a small adjustment. We need to raise an extra $50 million." An awkward pause followed. Box had previously raised $106 million, already a heady sum for a company with just $21 million in sales and no profits. Levie's early investor and biggest booster, Josh Stein of venture firm Draper Fisher Jurvetson, piped up: "I'm sorry, but you said $15 million, right?"

Nope. Five-oh.

A month earlier Levie, with the board's acquiescence, shot down a $600 million offer from virtual-computing giant Citrix. That would have given the guys in the room three to fifty times what they'd put into Box just a few years earlier. Now Levie was asking them to dilute their stake by some 15 percent. He hadn't even told his cofounder about it.

They should have seen it coming. Levie is on a mission, and it's an expensive one: to be the Oracle of the next generation of enterprise applications. Box is an online storage and collaboration service that finished 2013 with $124 million in revenue, double what it did in 2012, and five times bigger than in 2011. Levie figures he can keep growing quickly, but that's not interesting to him.

Instead, he wants to create a transformative technology company for the mobile era, one that will become the glue connecting any big company's myriad data and documents across all of its disparate software applications and makes them accessible securely on a tablet or phone. At that July 2011 board meeting Box already offered a better mobile experience than anything from Oracle, SAP, or Microsoft. But it had only five people selling to big companies, which put it at a crushing disadvantage to the giants.

A two-hour cross-examination later the board gave Levie the go-ahead to raise more cash to beef up the sales force, and he had no shortage of interest: His $50 million ask turned into an $81 million round, and then he raised another $150 million, at a valuation of $1.2 billion, and then yet another $100 million around Christmas 2013, which made the company worth almost $2 billion. All necessary, given the $169 million sales-obsessed Box lost in 2013, according to pre-IPO documents filed in early 2014.

Even Levie can't keep track of it all. "Sorry, which round am I talking about?" he asked, nervously cracking his knuckles. Levie is perpetually fidgeting with something—his iPhone, frizzy curls, jean cuffs, sneaker laces—in between sips of endless cups of black coffee. He generally rises at 10:20 a.m. and tends to fast through the work-day, taking his sole meal at dinner, after a half-hour power nap in his office lair, an 8-by-10 room with nothing but a scribble-filled white-board, purple couch, two orange earplugs, and an inhaler. He rarely drinks alcohol, even though he regularly schmoozes at wine-soaked business suppers, because after midnight is when he powers through e-mails before collapsing at 3:00 a.m.

His board has been accommodating to his ambition, in part be-cause of this work ethic and in part because he's taking the dilution along with them, betting together that they can make more owning less of something bigger. While his frenemy in the consumer online storage world, Drew Houston of Dropbox, has kept an estimated 15 percent stake, Levie is down to only 5.7 percent or so of Box, giving him a "mere" $100 million or so, pre-IPO, for his personal fortune. "My what?" he says, taking a mock puff of the inhaler. Levie's biggest extravagance: a BMW 3 Series he leased five years ago. "I'm living the life I dreamed of as a twelve-year-old. I don't have hobbies. I want to build a big company, and this is it."

HE'S CHOSEN A FORMIDABLE industry. Four companies founded decades ago—Microsoft, IBM, Oracle, and SAP—still control half of the software market, according to Gartner, which will soon eclipse $300 billion. All the others get scraps. The status quo consists of expensive licensing deals and even pricier setup costs followed by ongoing maintenance and consulting fees just to keep the software up to date. Yet the products they're selling are largely archaic. Most are stuck on servers talking to PCs and don't run on mobile devices, even though roughly half of American workers are using their smartphones for work and a surging number are also using tablets, per Forrester Research.

The new wave of more-convenient-to-own, cloud-based business software, which began last decade with Salesforce, Netsuite, and Workday, has swelled to dozens of startups now hitting the enterprise market with flexible pricing, mobile access, and tools that make doing business as easy as using Facebook. B2B software has also been a much healthier investment play. The IPOs of Workday and Splunk went off brilliantly while consumer Web firms Zynga and Groupon disappointed.

Levie built Box for this new world. A file stored in Box (this could be as simple as a Word document or as complex as a 3-D rendering of a new building) appears and can be shared (and in some cases edited) on any device with a browser. Box has apps on all the major mobile operating systems. His vision of IT's future cobbles together software from the new generation of players, with Box in the middle of it all acting as a data traffic cop, so that any piece of information from one offering can effortlessly be pulled from another application. In his world the expensive storage hardware and collaboration software "suites" from Microsoft, Hewlett-Packard, IBM, EMC, and NetApp go away.

Box's not-so-secret weapon is its freemium business model. With Box you get 5 gigabytes of online storage and basic features for nothing. If you want enhancements, better security, and IT-department-level controls, Box is as cheap as five dollars a month per person. Only 7 percent of the company's twenty million–plus users now pay the fee, but expansion of existing accounts is generating 40 percent annual revenue growth.

Box is already looking like the big-vision pitch Levie made to his investors back at that fateful board meeting. The company signed up four times as many annual deals worth over $50,000 in 2012 than it did in 2011, from companies like Gap, Electronic Arts, and Discovery, and by 2014 was cutting deals with the likes of General Electric. But while its human sales force has surged to a couple hundred, more than two-thirds of Box's deals originate when someone in an IT organization notices Box adoption and wants to wrap security and administrative controls around it.

The industry giants have noticed, too, and are quickly co-opting Levie's freemium, mobile-first approach. Salesforce launched its Facebook-for-business product, Chatter, with a freemium model in 2010. In 2012, Microsoft acquired Yammer, a freemium social-tool-for-business outfit, for $1.2 billion, citing the firm's business model as a reason for the purchase. And Google has made Google Docs a legitimate solution for business, as well. Meanwhile, Oracle, Microsoft, SAP, Netsuite, and Salesforce have lined up to partner with Box so that their salespeople have an answer to the inevitable customer question about getting data to the plethora of mobile devices that clutter a company's system.

All that action is what, literally, keeps Levie up at night. Says the now twenty-eight-year-old: "I have more gray hair than President Obama."

SOME OF THAT GRAY in his wavy tuft comes from a shockingly preternatural entrepreneurial career. Levie grew up on Mercer Island, Washington, a leafy suburb of Seattle where technology wealth from Microsoft and Amazon seemed to flow through the air. At eight years old he was distributing flyers offering himself for weed-pulling, dog walking, and anything else a neighbor might pay for. He turned ten the year Netscape was founded and spent his tweens browsing online, typically until 2:00 a.m., cooking up one new business idea a week, which he'd pitch to his father, Ben, a chemical engineer, and his mother, Karyn, a speech-language pathologist. "Honestly, it was tiresome," admitted Mom. "He even told me I should start a company with some tool that other speech pathologists need. I mean, I kind of stopped listening after a certain point."

His high school classmates were more enraptured. While he obsessed over the business models underpinning this new thing called the Internet, his buddy Jeff Queisser, who lived four houses down, would haul over his twenty-pound Dell tower and CRT monitor for all-night coding sleepovers. Some fifteen startups ensued. There was an Internet kiosk for hotels and malls, a Web portal for real estate listings, and "Zizap," which Levie described as a "really slow, pay-to-play search engine." They all failed, though Levie considers that word too binary: "Failure? I wouldn't put it that way. They didn't take off, sure, but I got something out of every one."

Besides lessons, he built a team. His Box cofounder and key hires all hail from Mercer Island High School: Queisser heads up technical operations, Dylan Smith is chief financial officer, Sam Ghods oversees technology, and Ashley Mayer is head of PR. "We weren't all buddies in high school," said Smith. "It was more that Aaron sought us out at some point and then united us in one of his many causes."

Levie squeezed his way with a low-B average into the University of Southern California as a business major. He exchanged startup ideas via e-mail with Smith, who was starting premed at Duke University. One was a sort of social network for college kids but limited to simply listing each student's interests. Levie also launched a site called socalendar.com, a directory of events in the L.A. area. It flopped.

But the idea that got them both excited popped up in a sophomore marketing class. Levie chose to research the online storage industry and instantly saw an attractive arbitrage opportunity. He could charge $2.99 a month for 1 gigabyte of storage that cost him only a dollar.

In 2005 he persuaded Smith to launch an online storage company that summer out of Smith's parents' attic on Mercer Island. They rented servers with Smith's $15,000 in online poker winnings to start it, then dropped off business prospectuses at the homes of Seattle's tech luminaries like Paul Allen and cold-called two dozen VCs. Not one bit. Then Mark Cuban changed everything. Levie had sent the dot-com billionaire and blogger a story pitch. Cuban's response: I want to invest. Six weeks later they had his check for $350,000 for 30 percent of the company. Levie and Smith decided to drop out of their respective colleges and head to Silicon Valley, driving Mrs. Levie's Nissan Quest to an uncle's backyard cottage in Berkeley.

Customers were signing up briskly, but Levie felt there was still too much friction in the act of pulling out a credit card to open a Box account. Some quick math showed they could give away the first gigabyte and make up the expense if only 3 percent of accounts upgraded to the $2.99-per-GB price, given that those paying customers were likely to eventually want loads of storage. In early 2006 Box moved to the "freemium" model, and overnight they hit fifty times the number of daily sign-ups. Great penetration—but also a frightful cash burn. Cuban wasn't happy with the equation, which mandated that investors subsidize the freeloaders in the hopes of making it up later.

That October the venture capital firm Draper Fisher Jurvetson came through with $1.5 million, some of which went to buy out Cuban entirely. While Cuban has built a multibillion fortune through some brilliantly timed moves, this one proved a disaster, as his stake today, even without investing another penny, would be worth upwards of $100 million.

Early on, though, it appeared Cuban would be proved right. Box came up shy of $500,000 in revenue in 2006, and while consumers were begging for new features, they weren't willing to pay for them. Rivals were dropping prices, and rumors began to swirl that Google and Apple would soon offer cloud storage for free.

Box was still a tiny operation. Its two cofounders and some of their high school crew slept on mattresses lining the floor of a garage next to their one-room Palo Alto office. Levie jumped on his share of support calls, which proved the ultimate market-research exercise. Many of their customers were "rogue" office workers, storing and collaborating on files in the cloud without their IT managers' approval. Levie would ask them what new features they wanted Box to add. Many said they would gladly pay one hundred times what Box was charging if it had security features and a dashboard that showed employee usage. Box, the office workers told Levie, was simpler to use than a similar Microsoft product called SharePoint. When Levie found out that SharePoint made Microsoft $2 billion a year, he realized he'd been targeting the wrong customers.

In one of the great "pivots" in recent Silicon Valley history, Box ditched the consumer play and became an enterprise software company in the middle of 2007. Again, he faced a dwindling pile of cash, and Draper Fisher wanted to see another investor buy-in before recommitting. Levie went to twenty venture capital firms, and none would touch Box because Levie's track record and knowledge of this new market were negligible, and the hoodie look that worked for Mark Zuckerberg fell flat. (His revised uniform: dark blazer, jeans, dress shirt, and neon Pumas.)

Levie finally found a believer in then twenty-nine-year-old Mamoon Hamid at U.S. Venture Partners. His $6 million infusion in January 2008 kept Box afloat for another year while the founders retuned their features for the corporate buyer, including the ability of administrators to delete accounts, track who accessed which file and when, and control which groups can have access to files and folders.

Levie turned himself into a student of enterprise software. He devoured industry classics like Thomas J. Watson Jr.'s *Father, Son & Co.*, about the early years of IBM, and Matthew Symonds' *Softwar*, an authorized Larry Ellison hagiography. "I immersed myself in it," said Levie. Literally: He lined the walls of his dingy apartment with four-foot-high posters of the logos of Oracle, Sun Microsystems, Salesforce, and Siebel Systems. (Though faded, they're still there. His girlfriend, who had been clerking for a federal judge in Arizona, "isn't here often enough to care," he said.)

A second epiphany came in April 2010 when Levie was sitting in his bedroom watching the live webcast of Steve Jobs unveiling the first iPad. "My imagination ran wild," Levie recalled. "The thing looked like a piece of paper, and that's exactly what most businesses are still running their businesses on." He instantly e-mailed Box's engineers, ordering them to develop an app for the device by the time it debuted in stores—and they did.

Around that same time Procter & Gamble started sniffing around. Executives at the consumer products giant were starting to use iPads and wanted access to their files. And while it took eighteen months of courting and customizing to close the deal, having a product that worked smoothly for 18,000 of its employees opened doors for Box at other giant companies.

Levie spent 2011 continuing his self-education. He e-mailed his favorite pioneers in his industry with a simple, if ballsy, request: "Spend one hour with me." Tom Siebel, who founded Siebel Systems (acquired by Oracle for $5.85 billion in 2005), told Levie he once traveled to four states in a single day to meet with customers. Craig Conway, who ran PeopleSoft when it sold to Oracle for $10.3 billion, glanced at Levie's calendar, saw roughly one customer meeting and echoed that advice. Levie, focused on what was going on inside Box, had lost the perspective, gleaned from IT support calls, that had saved the company. He began meeting eight customers a week, peppering each with questions about what was working and what wasn't.

This listening-tour process did more than hone Box's strategy. It honed Levie. The guy who turned off dozens of VCs is now considered a model entrepreneur. "We saw everything exactly the same way," said Gary Reiner, a partner at venture firm General Atlantic who spent months doing due diligence before putting $100 million into Box in 2012. "It's like he's been doing this for twenty years. I can't throw him a question he hasn't already thought of."

BOX'S LOS ALTOS HEADQUARTERS feel more like Facebook's fun zone than Oracle's stiff towers. There's a bright yellow slide, a room with ping-pong tables, unicorn figurines, and lots of scooters. "I'm not a scooter person, but this stuff matters for our culture," he said. Box's staff is approaching 1,000, with key hires from Oracle, Google, and Salesforce.

But for all the giddiness, danger lurks. Not a month goes by without some mortal threat against Box. Virtualization giant VMWare announced plans to offer file-synchronizing in 2012. Salesforce, an investor in Box, announced a rival storage feature called Chatterbox around the same time, though by 2013, it was already rebooting its effort. Dropbox, meanwhile, has started Dropbox for Business, in a play for those lucrative business accounts.

Then there's Microsoft, which has Box firmly in its sights. Levie got lucky by originally competing with the Redmond giant's Share-Point software. While Microsoft bundles it with other offerings and has sometimes threatened price hikes on existing products if customers signal they want to switch, SharePoint is notoriously expensive. For every $1 customers spend on the software itself, they're spending on average $8.70 for outside firms (developers and IT consultants) to get it to run. While it does considerably more than Box, such as linking into inventory systems, traditionally it's been hard to use and until recently didn't work on mobile devices running Google's Android system or Apple's iOS. The 900-pound gorilla, however, has woken up. "Box, along with other smaller companies, got there before Microsoft," said Jared Spataro, SharePoint's senior marketing director. "But we always see customers wanting fewer vendors, not more."

Levie's defenses, built in collaboration with his latest consigliere, Ben Horowitz, founding partner of the Valley's hottest VC shop, Andreessen Horowitz, which invested in Box's $48 million round in 2011, look like this: Build a sales team that can look and act like Oracle's while preserving Box's innovative, fast-moving culture, and make Box a viable platform on which other software firms can connect and sell their file-related technologies. The only way Levie will become the next Larry Ellison is to insert Box at the nexus of a company's most important data. "I have to do everything, all at once, as quickly as possible," said Levie, gleeful about the fact that he has bitten off more than he can chew. "If I had a clue how this industry worked, I would not attempt to do what we've done. I was blissfully ignorant."

CHAPTER 7

Jack Dorsey, Twitter, Square: Jack of All Trades

Jack Dorsey is arguably the most successful multitasker in business history. He cofounded two of the world's hottest tech companies almost on top of each other—simultaneously building himself a $1 billion fortune in each while serving as chairman of one and CEO of the other.

Twitter's story, of course, is widely known. Promotional platform, democracy tool, news disseminator—it's all that, and Dorsey's original microblogging vision, too. Twitter's post-IPO valuation has flirted with $40 billion. Unless you're a small business eager to accept credit cards, Square is less well-known and its outcome remains far less certain—though it's raised $200 million at valuations that, by 2014, had risen to $5 billion—given the huge competition emerging in mobile payments. But that's largely beside the point: When **Eric Savitz** spent time with him, the now-thirty-seven-year-old Dorsey was focused on the challenge that most successful entrepreneurs face: How does one allocate time so efficiently that a blockbuster can be achieved—multiple times?

———

You cover a lot of ground hanging out with Jack Dorsey. In just the first fifteen minutes of a visit to the San Francisco headquarters of Square, which makes the device that turns a smartphone into a credit/debit card machine, we covered the way he structures his time, how the company organizes work, a recent acquisition, group meetings, corporate transparency, and what he eats for breakfast every morning (two hard-boiled eggs with soy sauce). We darted into the company's cafe, where he insisted I try a Kombucha, a fermented tea energy drink. He urged me to try the grape version; bottles of the cherry variety, he explained, tend to explode. "You won't like it at first," he warned, correctly, of the vinegary brew.

Then we were off touring more of the third floor of the storied *San Francisco Chronicle* building. Dorsey looked over the shoulder of someone sitting in an open area among long rows of desks, plying a big-screen Mac, and then joined a discussion at a tall table between a group of graphic artists and marketing staffers. There are conference rooms—21 of them, all glass-enclosed, all named after notable squares, like Tahrir (Cairo), St. Peter's (Vatican City), and Old Market (Nottingham, where the legendary Robin Hood may or may not have hung out). In one darkened room a handful of engineers worked on integrating a large project with Starbucks, which invested $25 million in Square and now uses it to process all credit and debit transactions in its U.S. stores.

"We encourage people to stay out in the open because we believe

Sean Parker, Facebook

Drew Houston, DropBox

Elon Musk, Tesla Motors
and SpaceX

Kevin Systrom,
Instagram

Daniel Ek, Spotify

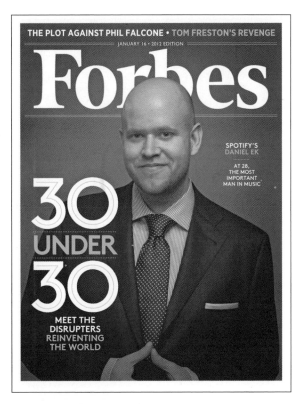

Aaron Levie, Box

Jack Dorsey, Twitter, Square

David Karp, Tumblr

Nick Woodman, GoPro

Brian Chesky, Airbnb

Alex Karp, Palantir

Pejman Nozad, angel investor

Evan Spiegel,
Snapchat

Adi Tatarko, Houzz

Palmer Luckey, Oculus Rift

Jan Koum, WhatsApp

in serendipity—and people walking by each other teaching new things," said Dorsey with a slight wave of his hand. "But every now and then you need to focus as one team."

This philosophical entrepreneur evokes a little bit of another technology wizard with mystical leanings. But Dorsey is nerdier than Steve Jobs (he is a programmer first, an impresario second), his ego seemingly in check. Like Jobs, Dorsey is a disrupter on an epic scale and a repeat offender. Twitter, the microblogging service he co-founded in 2006, has turned more than 500 million people world-wide into broadcasters of messages capable of starting revolutions. And by accepting e-payments with Square, more than two million businesses are upending the financial services industry; in 2013, Square exceeded $500 million in revenue.

Those companies have made Dorsey a billionaire. His stake in Twitter, after the 2013 IPO, was worth more than $1 billion. In that same year, his share of Square, based on funding valuations, also neared a billion.

Before he cocreated two of hottest tech companies on the planet, Dorsey gave little sign of brilliant focus. He wrote dispatch software for ambulances and cop cars, dropped out of college (twice), took up botanical drawing, became a certified masseur and, later, dabbled in fashion design. More recently he has made noises about becoming mayor of New York City. His mother sometimes despaired he would ever find himself.

But he knew better. The side trips are part of the road map; his discursiveness is the obverse of intense discipline. Dorsey is a serial wanderer, mentally and physically, because it helps him concentrate: "The best thinking time is just walking." He has worn a trench between Square, his previous apartment around the corner, and the offices of Twitter, a few blocks away. Before he starts his day, he runs three to five miles. He likes to take new recruits on tours of San Francisco.

Management by wandering around was made famous thirty years ago by *In Search of Excellence,* the book that celebrated the leadership and innovation of entrepreneurs like Bill Hewlett and David Packard. Dorsey has his own brand of "loose-tight properties"—autonomy on the shop floor but working under centralized values. Pay attention to the smallest things, Dorsey frequently says, while keeping sight of what's truly important.

The guy focuses not only on breakthrough ideas but also radically different kinds of corporate structures to contain and develop them. Wittingly or not, Dorsey provides an original model of how to start and run a company.

DORSEY GREW UP IN St. Louis, the oldest child of Tim and Marcia, who are clearly his biggest fans. In September 2013, they flew out to see their son speak at the Techonomy Detroit conference. And Jack, hardly innocent of the spotlight, confessed to pregame jitters backstage. Why? "My mom and dad are here."

Tim, who runs a small company called MA Tech Services, which makes mass spectrometers, reported that he is an avid Tweeter (@Tim535353). Jack's younger brothers tweet, too: There's Daniel (@darkside) and Andrew (@andrew), who writes on his home page, in blaring caps-lock-style, "U AINT COOL TILL U ON TWITTER."

Even Marcia tweets. @marciadorsey's page says: "Mother of @jack . . . Does that make me the grandmother of Twitter?"

As a kid Dorsey was captivated by iMaps and the cities they described. As a teen he became interested in the dispatch services used by taxi services and other transit systems. At sixteen Dorsey tried to start his own bicycle courier service, in part to have an excuse to write code to run the business—until he found little demand for bike messengers in St. Louis.

A self-taught coder, Dorsey graduated in 1995 from Bishop Du-Bourg High School, then enrolled at the University of Missouri-Rolla but didn't stay long. Still fascinated by systems, Dorsey discovered a security flaw in a website operated by a New York City company called Dispatch Management Services, run by Greg Kidd. Dorsey found Kidd's e-mail address on the company's computer system and sent him a note alerting him to the flaw. Kidd immediately offered Dorsey a job, and he bolted from Missouri for the Big Apple.

While in town, Dorsey enrolled at New York University. Though he's now clean-cut and often dressed in Prada suits, Dorsey in those days wore a nose ring and dreadlocks (he still sports tattoos under the expensive threads), and spent free time in the East Village listening to punk bands like Rancid. Kidd and Dorsey went on to start a new company called dNet, which provided same-day delivery of e-commerce purchases. dNet received early funding from the Band of Angels, a venerated group of one-hundred–plus Silicon Valley veterans, but the company never quite got traction. It was a good idea but a decade early: Amazon and Walmart now do the same thing.

After dNet flopped, Jack flew home to St. Louis, trained to be a massage therapist, and wound up following Kidd to the Bay Area. He settled into a tiny shed in the courtyard of Kidd's house in the Rockridge section of Oakland (Kidd says it was about 60 square feet but had power, broadband, and proximity to a hot tub). Dorsey spent his time helping take care of Kidd's infant daughter and then picked up work writing dispatch and ticketing software for an outfit providing ferry service to Alcatraz. That led to a full-time gig at the podcasting startup Odeo, built by a former Google star named Evan Williams.

Despite a wealth of buzz, Odeo never made it. "I didn't want to do podcasting at all, but I wanted to work with that team," said Dorsey, referring to Biz Stone and Williams. "We weren't building tools that we loved, or that we used, that we had to make better for ourselves."

But from that mess emerged something good, potentially great. Dorsey brought forward the seed idea for a microblog platform, and the group gave him a fortnight to write the code. "I took one other programmer named Florian [Weber] and Biz, and in two weeks we had it," he recalled. "Little by little, we took more employees from Odeo, and then eventually we spun it out as a separate company."

Not just any company. Twitter allowed Dorsey to focus on an idea instead of a business entity—an approach he would take again when launching Square. "I knew it would be a big concept, I knew it would have legs, because it was a concept and the essence of a technology that I was using in other modalities, dispatch, mainly," he said. "And then the company kind of just formed around it."

At the start, he says, he never even thought of Twitter as a company. It hardened into one, as a larva develops an exoskeleton. "The most efficient means to spread an idea today is a corporate structure; 200 years ago it was probably something different; 100 years from now it will be something completely different," he said. "But all of that is in service of the idea."

Twitter went viral at the South by Southwest conference in 2007 and has been soaring ever since. It raised over $1 billion in venture money, from the likes of Kleiner Perkins, DST Global, Union Square Ventures, Benchmark Capital, and others. And then its November 2013 IPO saw shares soar—Twitter was suddenly worth almost $25 billion.

DORSEY, STILL REGARDED AS a coder rather than a manager, was kicked upstairs at Twitter in 2008, retaining the chairman's job but stepping away from day-to-day management. Rather than take a break or remain content helping to guide Twitter, he immediately jumped in yet again. Dorsey launched Square from his one-bedroom apartment overlooking the old U.S. Mint in San Francisco with Jim McKelvey, who had hired him as a programming summer intern when Dorsey was fifteen. The idea for a new company grew out of a practical problem. McKelvey, a sometime glassblower, had designed a $2,500 faucet but failed to make the sale because he couldn't process a credit card.

Twitter has gotten credit for helping to topple Arab dictators. Square's plan was to disrupt the multitrillion-dollar payments system. Originally called Squirrel (as in squirreling money away), Square set out to make it far easier for small merchants to accept plastic, with a smartphone peripheral that can swipe cards, for a 2.75 percent transaction fee. (Square forks over most of that to credit card companies.) In a new twist, Square started offering merchants the option of paying $275 a month for unlimited transactions up to $250,000 a year.

Dorsey "looked at how money could be a lot more functional," says Vinod Khosla, the venture capitalist, who invested in Square's Series A round. "That's a different question than the one PayPal is asking. It's a more fundamental question: What can you do for the users of money?"

Square is not just about transactions. Dorsey wanted to help retailers run their businesses more efficiently by giving them better data—and getting closer to their customers. A service called Square Register turns a mobile device or tablet into a point-of-sale system, providing inventory management, customer tracking, business analytics, and the like. The next innovation, Square Wallet, lets you buy things without having to swipe a card; you can even pay hands-free at certain businesses, including Starbucks, using localization technology that tells a store you're there. Square Wallet also allowed retailers to build in rewards programs.

It was a huge potential market, with huge competition, including PayPal, credit card companies, and, at some point, Apple. And a huge entrepreneurial challenge for Dorsey, who still had responsibilities at Twitter. To fulfill his dreams for the company, Dorsey developed an unusual corporate organism at Square—and a highly structured approach to managing his time. "The company needs to have a weekly cadence," he explained. Dorsey's schedule looks something like this:

— Monday: address management issues
— Tuesday: product engineering and design
— Wednesday: marketing and communications, and growth
— Thursday: meetings with outside partners and developers
— Friday: "company and culture" and recruiting

— Saturday: off (in particular, he likes to hike)

— Sunday: strategic thinking and job interviews

For a while Dorsey stuck to this schedule every week at both Twitter and Square. In 2012, he began going to Twitter just every other day, mainly to discuss strategy.

How did such militaristic discipline allow for spontaneity—and discovery? "I do a lot of my work at stand-up tables, which anyone can come up to," Dorsey said. "And I get to hear all these conversations around the company. I spend 90 percent of my time with people who don't report to me, which also allows for serendipity, since I'm walking around the office all the time. You don't have to schedule serendipity. It just happens."

Dorsey's model for the well-tuned company is a newsroom. He once worked on his high school newspaper, and sees himself as the editor-in-chief of Square, curating ideas that come from his staff and suggesting ideas to them. "I really like that model at both Twitter and Square because it allows for people with the most information around the company to bubble something up," he said. "But it also allows the leaders in our company to recognize trends and intersections, and [assign] teams to those intersections." Employees, Dorsey says, "can actually dramatically change the course of the company by presenting a good idea."

Transparency and trust drive everything. Dorsey insists that everyone who works for him knows what the company is up to and why it's doing it. So he instituted an astonishing rule at Square: At every meeting involving more than two people, someone must take notes—and send them to the entire staff.

It doesn't matter what the meeting is about: bug fixes, new partnerships, pending contracts, a new launch, important metrics. Everyone hears about them. Dorsey says he often gets thirty to forty meeting notes every day. He filters them in his in-box and reads them through on his iPhone when he gets home at night.

More incredible is that with such massive scads of sensitive information circulating to the 400-plus people at Square, not a single item has surfaced on the Web. When Starbucks CEO Howard Schultz reached Dorsey about using Square to process all credit and debit transactions in 7,000 stores, he announced the tentative discussions at an all-hands meeting hours later. No one tweeted the news. "We've had zero leaks, zero leaks," said Dorsey, knocking twice on a table, "since day one of the company."

ON A FRIDAY AT Square, just days after acquiring a New York–based Web designer called 80/20 in October 2013, Dorsey sketched the program for his weekly all-hands meeting, called Town Square, at 5:05 p.m. "We have drinks, we have pizza," he said. "Today we're having hot dogs because we're celebrating New York." The event kicked off with Jay-Z's "Empire State of Mind" and the introduction of twenty-four new team members from 80/20, and concluded with Sinatra's version of "New York, New York." In between Dorsey presented a recap of what he had told Square's directors earlier in the week. "We're going to show the whole company everything we presented to the board and all their comments."

Is Dorsey thinking beyond Twitter and Square? "I do believe in the power of threes, so conceptually I would love a third company," he mused. Such as? Well, he has an abiding interest in education and health care. Or something else, perhaps. "I don't think there has been any recent revolution of our government or how we think about running governments," he said. "I would love to see technology help with that."

CHAPTER 8

David Karp, Tumblr:
The $1 Billion Art Project

Even among a peer group of digital mavericks that comes in all shapes and sizes (as long as you're male), David Karp physically stands out. Beneath a Ringo-esque mop of brown hair grows a six-foot-one, 140-pound beanpole, with arms that resemble a praying mantis. To address the gangliness, the Tumblr founder wears button-downs, with the sleeves rolled up past his elbows. (When we shot him for the cover of *Forbes* in a suit, our fashion director Joseph DeAcetis actually cut the arms off his shirt and pulled them down so that the cuffs would show behind the coat—a tale that went viral for a couple days after *Esquire* detailed it.) And there's a thoughtfulness and sweetness that accompany the adolescent build. Let there be no mistake: Amid these sharks, Karp is the artist, one consistently ambivalent about making money. Still, when you build something that people want in this era, the cash will find you, a fact that **Jeff Bercovici** discovered as he spent time with Karp and Tumblr throughout 2012. By May 2013, Yahoo had swallowed his company whole, paying more than $1 billion—and giving Karp, the artist, almost $100 million in additional incentives to finish his masterpiece.

———

David Karp was in the midst of a rite of passage that seems universal for the young tycoons of the Internet's social era: He was buying himself a proper swank pad. And like Mark Zuckerberg's luxe but dowdy $6 million manse in Palo Alto and Sean Parker's $20 million Greenwich Village carriage house-cum-party palace, Karp's choice said a lot about him—and Tumblr, the blogging platform he founded in 2007. The 1,700-square-foot, $1.6 million loft, which he then set about remodeling, is quite modest for a twenty-eight-year-old whose net worth exceeds $200 million. That's in part because it's located in the world's hipster capital, Williamsburg, Brooklyn, where irony trumps showiness—he's quite likely the richest person in the neighborhood. But the most telling feature was on the inside, which contained . . . virtually nothing. A spartan bedroom with a half-empty closet. A living room area with nothing but a sofa and a TV. (One concession to opulence: a restaurant-grade kitchen for his girlfriend, Rachel Eakley, a trained chef.) "I don't have any books. I don't have many clothes," Karp shrugged. "I'm always so surprised when people fill their homes up with stuff."

"He owns, like, three items," confirmed Marco Arment, Karp's first and, for a long time, only employee at Tumblr. "He's always looking for ways he can get rid of something." Even Karp's person is spare in the extreme: His one suit, though trimly cut, flapped around his six-foot-one frame when he fidgeted, which he does a lot. Maybe it's all the calories he burns this way that keeps him skinny, like a teenager who has yet to fill out his bones. "I've always been forty pounds underweight," he said.

For Tumblr's CEO, minimalism isn't just an esthetic choice. It's the key to freedom. When he travels he avoids making plans more than a few days in advance, even on his trips to Japan, and packs only the sveltest of carry-ons. "It's my Jason Bourne or James Bond fantasy, wanting to be perfectly mobile," he said. Roelof Botha, a partner at the Silicon Valley venture firm Sequoia Capital and one of Tumblr's directors before its sale to Yahoo, recalled showing up at a board meeting in New York toting only "the tiniest of duffel bags" for his trip. "David took one look at me and said, 'You really brought all that stuff?' "

Karp's intolerance for the inessential permeates Tumblr. Where others looked at the twin revolutions of blogging and social networking and saw new tools for communication, Karp saw possibilities for making them radically easier and more intuitive. Tumblr lowered the bar to creating a beautiful, dynamic website and raised the payoff in the form of positive social reinforcement.

If Facebook is where you check in with your real-life friends and Twitter is how you keep up with current events, the Tumblr experience can be boiled down to people expressing themselves publicly. Like those other two networks, Tumblr is organized in the form of streams of posts. But it's far more sensory and emotive, a swirl of photographs, songs, inside jokes, animated cartoons and virtual warm fuzzies. On the main Tumblr feed compiled by its editors, a photojournalist's visual diary of Afghanistan might be followed by a cartoonist's impressionistic drawings of Darth Vader, which give way to a gallery of hamsters that look like President Obama.

Users make sense of the chaos with the aid of a dashboard, the interface for finding and following other users and keeping track of the feedback their posts receive. Hearts are good; "reblogs" are better, suggesting another user liked your post enough to share it with his or her followers. The tools for creating these multimedia posts are simple: seven buttons that let you add text, photos, hyperlinks, video, music, dialogues, or quotes with a click.

The result: classic hockey-stick growth. In November 2012 it shouldered its way into the top ten online destinations, edging out Microsoft's Bing and drawing nearly 170 million visitors to its galaxy of user-created pages, according to the measurement firm Quantcast. Since then, the number of blogs on the site has more than doubled, to 182 million—these registered users create 100 million new posts every day (the cumulative total for the site is approaching 100 billion). Its final funding round, in September 2011, valued Tumblr at $800 million. When the company looked to raise a new round of investment in the spring of 2013, Yahoo stepped in with its acquisition offer, worth a bit over $1 billion, making Karp's approximately 25 percent stake worth around $250 million.

For Karp, that wasn't the end of the story; it was just the beginning. Yahoo locked him up for four years with a cash-and-stock package worth another $81 million. Tumblr now faces three challenges: to prove that it can continue the growth. That it can actually make money. And that David Karp, the creative genius and quintessential minimalist, is the right guy to lead Tumblr to long-term glory. "The road is littered with dead companies that made the wrong move at the wrong time, the MySpaces of the world," said Gartner analyst Brian Blau, shortly before the Yahoo deal. "They've got to be really careful."

Karp has momentum. When Hurricane Sandy flooded massive data centers in New York, knocking the Huffington Post, Gawker, and BuzzFeed offline, all three gravitated to Tumblr as their temporary publishing platform. Hollywood has taken note, with four different network TV projects adapted from viral Tumblr blogs. And this: When Oxford Dictionaries USA designated "GIF" its word of the year for 2012, it credited Tumblr with pushing the term, a technical name for a type of compressed image file, into the mainstream. "The growth we've seen in the last year just totally overshadows everything that came before it," said Karp. "To be honest, it's a place I never thought we'd be."

And, in some ways, never hoped to be. Tumblr is growing up and, as anyone with a baby or a mortgage can tell you, that means expensive complications. "The pressure on Internet media companies to deliver revenues is going way, way up," said Gawker Media owner Nick Denton. Karp, who once showed disdain for advertising, finally allowed ads on Tumblr in 2012, and it finished the year with $13 million in bookings, according to the research firm PrivCo. In 2013, it hoped for a "leap" year, with revenues of $100 million, but that didn't happen: Yahoo has said its sales are still "not meaningful" enough to be worth reporting.

The acquisition relieves some of the immediate pressure to show a profit, but Yahoo's patience won't be infinite. Investors expect CEO Marissa Mayer to juice the company's long-stalled revenue growth, and she has made it clear that Tumblr, under Karp, is a big part of her plan for doing so.

WHEN HE STARTED DOWN the path that led to Tumblr, Karp was just another teenager obsessed with tech and too smart even for his elite public high school, New York City's Bronx Science. Karp's mother, a teacher on Manhattan's Upper West Side, and his father, a musician, knew their son, the older of two boys, needed more avenues to pursue his interests. So his mom approached Fred Seibert, a family friend whose children she taught. A longtime executive at MTV Networks and Hanna-Barbera, Seibert was running his own animation production company. "David's mom said, 'Fred, your business has computers in it, right?'" Seibert recalled. " 'You know, my fourteen-year-old is really interested in computers. Could he come by and visit?' "

"I was terrified," Karp said of that first meeting. But his fascination with the work of the engineers outweighed his trepidation, and the visits became regular until, Seibert recalled, "One day he said, 'I can come by every day now—I'm going into home schooling.'" That, he decided after crunching admissions statistics, was his best shot at getting into MIT—which he in turn had determined was the best launching pad for computer engineers. He also began taking classes in Japanese at the Japan Society and seeing a math tutor, with whom he worked on writing software for winning at blackjack and poker.

But MIT was not in the cards. By the time his peers were writing application essays, Karp was working as head of product at the parenting website UrbanBaby. After CNET acquired the site in 2006, Karp used the proceeds from the sale of his shares to start his own little for-hire development firm, Davidville, where he also dabbled in creating products of his own. While he'd built a multiuser blogging platform for Seibert's company, he wasn't satisfied with it. "One day he came by and said, 'This blogging thing is really hard. Isn't it too hard?' " recalled Seibert, who had no idea what Karp was talking about. Knowing he was out of his depth, Seibert turned to one of his own investors, Bijan Sabet of Spark Capital.

"Fred called me up and said, 'Hey, you've got to spend more time with David. He's unbelievably talented,'" Sabet remembered. They got together, and Karp showed him a Web application he'd invented that made creating and sharing all kinds of digital content—text, photos, videos, hyperlinks—remarkably simple. It was Tumblr. "I was just blown away," said Sabet. "I hadn't seen anything that beautifully designed."

But getting Karp to commit to it as a business was tough. He "didn't want to be known as a business guy. David didn't conceive of Tumblr as anything other than a tool he wanted for making his life better," said Seibert. "He exhibited a passion early on, but it wasn't a passion for building a business."

"I basically spent the summer of 2007 trying to talk him into starting a company around it," added Sabet. "He was like, 'Hey, I like my consulting company.' But he was also intrigued about start-ups." When Sabet brought Karp his first term sheet for a proposed venture investment, Karp balked, saying it was "too much money with too much pressure." But when the kitty was reduced to $750,000 at a valuation of $3 million, led by Spark and the famously founder-friendly Union Square Ventures, Karp allowed himself to be persuaded.

Or, partly so, as Karp had to be talked out of his initial reluctance on a lot of fronts. As Tumblr grew from embryo to leviathan, he had to learn to subordinate his own instincts and inclinations to those of Seibert, Sabet, and his other investors, whom he refers to collectively as "my mentors" and speaks of only in the most complimentary of ways, even when disagreeing with them.

One focus of disagreement was over Tumblr's proper size. In its first year it was a two-man shop, Karp and Arment, whom Karp recruited via a Craigslist ad. In April 2008 they hired Marc LaFountain to handle user support, but he was in Virginia, and it took over a year before he met either of them in person. "So even when he had an employee, it didn't feel like we did," said Arment.

Around this time Karp told Sabet he'd been looking at the organizational structures of other digital media companies, from Craigslist, which had twenty-six people, to MySpace and Facebook, which each employed roughly 1,000. "And he says, 'I could do it with four people for the rest of my life,' and he really believed it," said Sabet.

But reality bit. As Tumblr's user base climbed into six and seven figures, the site increasingly had stability issues. Product fixes and improvements got stuck in a bottleneck. "We were getting overwhelmed," said Arment.

"I was a little too clever at times," Karp acknowledged. "The fact that I didn't have the foresight to build out a bigger engineering team earlier cost us some serious months. The reason we're so much more productive today is we've got people now who've been through this stuff before."

But there's a trade-off. The bigger Tumblr gets, the more time Karp spends doing things that don't play to his strengths: Schmoozing clients, dazzling analysts, navigating the politics of Yahoo, raising the fear of God with his troops—these don't come easily to the reserved Karp. "We've never seen him angry," said Rick Webb, who helped run a digital marketing agency, the Barbarian Group, before joining Tumblr as its "revenue consultant."

For years most business-side duties were handled by John Maloney, whom Karp had hired as Tumblr's first president after working for him at UrbanBaby. But as the company took on executives to oversee those areas, Maloney told Karp he was ready to leave. "There weren't a lot of politics around it," said Maloney. "It got to the point that there were a lot of people in the room. I wanted to go and do my own thing." He left in 2012, with Karp taking over his reports.

These days what keeps Karp up at night isn't buggy code but "team stuff. Am I being a good enough leader for these guys? Am I giving them everything they deserve and setting this up as a collaborative, positive environment? When it feels like it's slightly off, it's all I can think about until I fix it."

After Maloney left, insiders discussed bringing in a bigger-league version of him, à la Sheryl Sandberg at Facebook—adult supervision, leaving Karp free to focus on product strategy and vision. "David's smart enough that if he needed to manage, he could, but he doesn't relish that, so why put him in that box?" asked Sequoia's Botha. The board was still interviewing prospective candidates when the Yahoo deal rendered it moot.

Added Botha: "Tumblr wouldn't be Tumblr without David. He needs to be a part of the core business if we're going to make this a spectacular success."

FOR TUMBLR—AND YAHOO, WHICH bet $1 billion on Karp—spectacular success now boils down to one metric: profits. As recently as 2009 it was still trendy to doubt whether advertising or commerce could thrive on social platforms or whether users would rebel at intrusions into their personal conversations and creepy behavioral targeting.

For all its well-documented growing pains, Facebook has proven social's revenue efficacy several times over—when it first crossed into the black in 2009 and, more recently, when it revealed that its nascent advertising efforts on mobile are already driving more than half of its $8 billion in annual revenue. Twitter, while smaller, is on a similar trajectory, with $665 million in ad revenues in 2013.

Tumblr, said Sabet, is "where Twitter was two or three years ago." Now the company has to evolve into a sales machine, something that's clearly not Karp's forte: While no longer a teenage shoe gazer, he's still too shy and introverted for the table-pounding, back-slapping role. That explains why Tumblr, before the Yahoo deal, poached Groupon's Lee Brown, a ten-year Yahoo vet, to become its head salesman and armed him with a dozen sellers, focused on bringing in sponsors like AT&T, GE, and American Apparel. In February 2014, Yahoo announced that Tumblr's sponsored posts would become the focus of the parent company's native advertising strategy across all its properties ("native" being industry lingo for seamless, non-interruptive marketing messages).

Before Karp lifted his ad ban, the only real monetization of Tumblr came from other people. More than 100 writers have leveraged their Tumblr blogs into books, and several have scored TV deals, including Lauren Bachelis, whose *Hollywood Assistants* was adapted by CBS, and Emma Koenig, whose *F—k! I'm in My Twenties* went into development at NBC. (Neither project ultimately made it to air.) Commerce within Tumblr has mostly revolved around the creation and licensing of design "themes" for users looking to spruce up their pages. "For the people who are making those themes, it's incredibly lucrative," said Chris Mohney, who was editor-in-chief of the in-house news organ Storyboard, which shut down in 2013. But it's less so for Tumblr itself, whose cut of the sales added up to less than $5 million annually, reports the research firm PrivCo.

But if Tumblr's early moneymaking efforts were modest, its ambitions are outsized. Karp proposes to reinvent Internet advertising all over again and to do it while eschewing the path blazed by Google, Facebook, and Twitter.

In his critique of those companies' offerings, the normally polite-to-a-fault Karp doesn't pull punches. "Hyper-hyper-targeting of little blue links" is how he dismisses them. In 2010 he made headlines by publicly declaring that Web advertising "really turns our stomachs" and would never wind up on his network, a remark Karp's nervous investors have been urging him to explain now that the division's sales reps have started calling on Madison Avenue.

Here's what he said he meant: Those "little blue links" are effective, but only in the most limited way, at the narrow end of the so-called purchase funnel. "It's about grabbing you at the moment you're ready to buy," said Karp. Google, Facebook, and Twitter can use a combination of behavioral targeting and borrowed social relevance to do that with a high degree of success, but they have little effect on consumers' attitudes and emotions. That's the job of so-called brand advertising.

Right now, despite the great migration of time and money to the Internet, almost all brand messaging occurs in traditional media, especially TV. "There's $50 billion in brand, but none of it's really on the Web," added Tumblr's revenue guy Webb.

The spenders of that $50 billion, Karp says, are awaiting digital advertising formats whose artistry and expression forge an emotional connection with consumers—the sort, romanticized in *Mad Men* and celebrated in Super Bowl commercials, that can make them laugh, cry, or call their mothers.

The same tools that make Tumblr a favored medium for creative types make it the ultimate blank canvas for marketers. What brands pay for isn't the ability to create content—that's free for anyone—but the ability to promote it in the form of sponsored mobile or Web posts. They can also pay to have brands promoted in Spotlight (an accounts-to-follow suggestion) or Radar (editors' picks). Together these two venues generate more than 120 million impressions per day. The vast majority goes to organically popular content, but 5 percent to 20 percent of those are made available for paid promotion. Rates are relatively high: The cost for a thousand impressions (CPM) ranges from $4 to $7, pushing into the premium end of the digital ad market. (Facebook's CPMs range from 30 cents for small, generic banners to almost $10 for certain types of social ads delivered over mobile devices.)

Ad agency Droga5 used Tumblr to promote the launch of Kraft's new, youth-targeted chewing gum brand, iD. One piece of content created for the campaign, an animated GIF of a dinosaur, was promoted through Radar and got more than 40,000 interactions, according to Chet Gulland, the agency's head of digital strategy. About half were "reblogs," meaning users essentially reposted the ads on their own pages and shared them with their friends. "It was really exciting to have a platform like that where you could reach a huge audience of exactly the right people and they seem so willing to engage with it," he said.

The iD campaign also ran on Facebook, which, like Tumblr, charges for the ability to promote content. But recent changes to the algorithm governing Facebook's main news feed have made it harder for brands to get their content seen without paying for extra promotion; some have likened this to extortion. In an angry blog post about the changes, Dallas Mavericks owner Mark Cuban cited Tumblr as a platform that brands should consider as an alternative to Facebook's strong-arm tactics. "David has done a great job of making Tumblr a staple of younger demographics, to the point where for many it's replacing Facebook as a day-to-day destination," said Cuban. (The two are acquaintances.)

Another key difference is privacy. Whereas Facebook exploits users' data to target them with specific ads, Tumblr is less invasive. "We don't want to get mired in that crazy, scary privacy world Facebook is in," said Webb. "That's a big red line for us."

A dotted line, perhaps: After merging into Yahoo and gaining access to its ad-serving technology, Tumblr finally started using users' location and gender to target sponsored posts. But even were Tumblr to match Facebook's degree of behavioral-targeting wizardry, it's doubtful it could ever come close to its audience, much less its revenue. Whereas Mark Zuckerberg's company strives to "make the world more open and connected," Tumblr's motto invites users to "Follow the world's creators." Catering to artists gave Tumblr an identity and a ready-made market but, in the long run, it's measured in the hundreds of millions, not billions, of members. The whole world may not need a Tumblr. "I do sort of wonder how they're going to transition from where they are today," said Gartner's Blau. "Tumblr has to change the perception that they're only for the creative crowd."

The key challenge for Tumblr going forward is the same one confronting every social network phenomenon: how successfully it can accommodate an audience that is rapidly transitioning from laptops and desktops to tablets and smartphones—and learn to make money off it. Though Tumblr's minimalist design and intuitive navigation leave it better positioned for the move, it's still a critical juncture. "This company was born on the Web," said Sabet. "It was not a mobile-first company, as it were."

Low-rated mobile apps that were initially outsourced have been redone in-house and now receive much higher ratings from users. Though Tumblr still hasn't quite figured out how some of its most popular features, like a browser bookmarklet that streamlines the sharing of Web pages, translate into the app universe, time spent on its mobile app is growing three times as fast as on the Web.

Karp's a quick study on this. Besides, his mentors aren't afraid to give him a good, hard correction when they think he needs one. "For all my learning how to be a CEO, I've made way fewer mistakes," he said, thanks to "that support system I really trusted who could grab me by the back of the sweater and say, 'David, you should pay attention.'"

These days, when Karp gets the urge to tinker, he doesn't dive into code. Instead, he rolls up his sleeves and works on one of his three motorcycles. While that may seem to violate his rule against accumulating stuff, he likes how simple they are compared with cars. Almost no one can fix his own jalopy anymore, but with bikes, he said, "it's all hanging out. Anything you want to get to, you can just pull it out and work on it." Plus, you can't have more than one backseat driver.

CHAPTER 9

Nick Woodman, GoPro: Chasing the Thrillionaire

It's hard to get too jealous of Sean Parker, Drew Houston, and other hacker prodigies, who took to computers the way Mozart took to piano. But then there's Nicholas Woodman, the surfer dude who decided that he really needed to figure out how to take pictures of himself on the waves with a disposable camera. He's now a billionaire and not yet forty. The GoPro founder is also an apt reminder of two things: First, that technology has blown everything wide open. An idea that only Eastman Kodak could have pulled off a generation ago—assuming, of course, their corporate-think could have even conjured it—can now be executed by a kid with his mom's sewing kit and the phone number for a random manufacturer in China. (A huge dose of social media doesn't hurt.) Second, pluck is as important as brains. Woodman was so determined to make GoPro work that he fed himself intravenously and peed out the window, saving the time needed to walk to the kitchen and bathroom. **Ryan Mac** got to see this man-teen's determination firsthand in 2013, from the slopes of Montana to the waves of Mavericks to the skies over California wine country.

———

Nick Woodman turned thirty-nine in 2014. His constantly tousled sepia hair and permanent, mischievous half-grin make him look twenty-nine. And he acts nineteen, as I learned 30,000 feet above the Rocky Mountains, after Woodman packed me, his wife, Jill, and a dozen of his favorite colleagues and buds into a chartered Gulfstream III en route to Montana's Yellowstone Club, the most exclusive ski hill in the U.S.

Already hopped up on Red Bull, tempered by a liter of coconut water, Woodman darted about the cabin, occasionally breaking conversation to unleash his trademark excited wail that friends liken to a foghorn. "YEEEEEEEEEEEEEOW." A flight attendant emerged with breakfast on a silver platter. "You know what the best thing about morning ski trips is?" he asked the cabin rhetorically. "McDonald's!" And with that he inhaled a McGriddle in all of three bites.

The man-teen routine was more than an act: It's the recipe for how he's become one of America's youngest billionaires. A decade ago, Woodman craved a camera he could strap to his wrist so that his buddies could see his surfing exploits. The result is GoPro, America's fastest-growing digital imaging company.

Go anywhere active, whether it's the mountains of Vail or the scuba-diving depths of Honolulu's Hanauma Bay, and you're bound to see a GoPro or twenty. Kids these days don't film their wave rides or half-pipe tricks. They GoPro them, strapping the $200 to $400 cameras to helmets, handlebars, and surfboards. The cinema-grade, panoramic "point-of-view" footage that comes out of a GoPro transforms mere mortals into human highlight reels, without blowing a huge hole in the budget. Shaun White, who says he used to tape old cameras to his hand, used GoPros on his runs during the 2014 Winter Olympics. Hollywood directors, including Michael Bay, keep crates of them on set. The NFL has tested them in their end zone pylons to capture touchdown replays. The Rolling Stones deployed them on stage. Police forces and the U.S. military have started to incorporate the cameras into training exercises. Woodman, who calls it a "life" camera, proved the point by wearing one on his chest during the hospital deliveries of both his sons. On the plane to Montana, Woodman's GoPro crew rigged their devices in every cranny in the cabin, including on the pilots' heads, to document their journey.

Up until 2013, GoPro sales doubled every year since the first camera's debut in 2004 and it now accounts for about 45 percent of all digital camcorder sales in the United States. In 2013 the company sold 3.8 million cameras and grossed $1 billion. Impressive numbers that fueled a succesfull June 2014 IPO that raised $430 million.

Even prior to that, Woodman had already made his nut. Chinese electronics manufacturer Hon Hai Precision Co., better known as Foxconn, the guys who make zillions of iPhones, made a $200 million investment in GoPro in December 2012. That valued the San Mateo, California firm at $2.25 billion and shot Woodman onto the *Forbes* World's Billionaires list. Following GoPro's IPO, he still owned a little under 50 percent. His net worth now hovers around $2.5 billion.

It's a head-spinning turn of events for a Peter Pan, still south of forty, running a billion-dollar technology company. As he barreled through Yellowstone's freshly groomed powder in a pea-green helmet, it's clear Woodman has found bliss. "YEEEEEEEEEEEEEEOW," he howled from his bloodied and chapped lips as he GoPro'd his every turn.

AS THE YOUNGEST OF four children, Woodman has always been something of a schemer. Growing up in Silicon Valley's prosperous Atherton (his father brokered Pepsi's purchase of Taco Bell), he was, as his teachers recall, a "supremely confident" boy who wasn't afraid to challenge those in charge. "There was always a smile on his face, either a great big one or a kind of sly, smirky thing," said Craig Schoof, Woodman's former baseball coach and history teacher. "There was the, 'Yeah, I'm happy,' or the 'Yeah, I'm happy, and I'm planning something.'" He once made a fiver by betting a biology teacher he could run a mile under six minutes (he ran it in 5:40).

Woodman focused more on sports than books, maintaining a B+ average and copping a middling SAT score. He eventually became wave-obsessed, attending the University of California, San Diego because of its proximity to sunshine and salt water. "I remember my parents not being very supportive of it," he said. "But if I didn't follow my passion for surfing . . . I would have never come up with the concept to make a wrist camera."

That concept came a few years after college after an online gaming service he started, Funbug, went belly-up in the dot-com crash of 2000–2001, taking with it $3.9 million of investors' money. "I'd never failed at anything before except computer science engineering classes," he said. "So it was like, 'Holy shit, maybe I'm not capable of doing this.' "

To get his head straight again, Woodman lit out on a surf odyssey through Australia and Indonesia, one last big trip before what he figured would become a life of comfortable middle-class monotony. He brought a contraption he'd made out of a broken surfboard leash and rubber bands that allowed him to dangle a Kodak disposable camera to his wrist for easy operation when the perfect wave hit. Close friend and current GoPro creative director Brad Schmidt met Woodman in Indonesia and became one of the first to toy with the strap. One of his first observations: Woodman needed a camera durable enough to take the wear and tear of the sea. Five months into being a surf bum, a recharged Woodman returned to California with the seed of an idea.

Woodman, then twenty-seven, holed up in the house he shared in Moss Beach, California, just over the hills from Silicon Valley. He "checked out" from his normal life, including friends and family, locking himself in his beachside bedroom to build his first prototypes. Deciding that he had to sell the strap, the camera, and the casing, he armed himself with a drill and his mother's sewing machine and, strapped on a CamelBak filled half with Gatorade and half with water (negating the thirty-second walk to the kitchen) for eighteen-hour work sessions. "I'd have a sliding door to the outside so I could just go take a pee out on the bushes out on the side," Woodman recalled. He gave himself four years to make it work before he would drop his idea and enter the workforce. "I was so scared that I would fail again that I was totally committed to succeed."

"After he took off, he was like, 'I think I'm going to start this wrist strap company for surfers,' " said Schmidt, who was skeptical.

Added Woodman: "I thought to myself, 'If I made a few hundred grand a year, I'm, like, in heaven.'"

Between sewing together old wetsuit material and drilling holes in raw plastic, Woodman was constantly trolling online and at trade shows for a camera he could modify and license as his own. He settled on a $3.05 35-millimeter model made in China, sending his plastic cases and $5,000 on a prayer to an unknown entity named Hotax. Woodman received his 3-D models and renderings a few months later and sold his first product in September 2004 at an action-sports trade show in San Diego.

That was the first validation for Woodman, whose friends thought their former surfing buddy had held his breath underwater for a little too long. Neil Dana, his roommate and first hire, recalls a work-obsessed guy constantly fixated on success. "We would be at a party," Dana recalled, "and he would come up the stairs and be like, 'Dude, check this out, this is how we're going to become millionaires!'" Woodman was only three zeroes off.

GoPro grossed $350,000 in its first full year of sales. Woodman was the all-in-one product engineer, R&D head, salesman, and packaging model. He and Dana rang up surf shops across the country hoping to get some of their product out of Woodman's father's home in Sausalito and into the market. In 2005 he appeared on QVC three times, running into Spanx founder and fellow future billionaire Sara Blakely while she was building her company as well. ("If she remembers me, I'll be amazed," said Woodman. "But I'd love to get word to her to give her a digital high-five on crushing it.")

Woodman eschewed venture capital as he grew—a by-product of his Funbug experience and a desire to work without suits interfering. Said Dana, "He wanted to keep it private for as long as possible so he could get a Lotus for 'product testing' and do things and not have to answer to a board about it." At the outset Woodman dropped in $30,000 of his own money, as well as $35,000 from his mother and two $100,000 investments from his father. The company made money from that point on and today boasts gross profit margins of about 37 percent, as of the end of 2013. It wasn't until May 2011 that GoPro took on $88 million from five venture firms, including Riverwood Capital, led by former Flextronics CEO Michael Marks, and Steamboat Ventures, Disney's venture investment arm, which allowed him, his family, and some early executives to take a good chunk of cash out.

That's how Woodman can now fly via G-III, versus the days he spent sleeping out in his 1971 Volkswagen bus or driving Penske trucks to set up trade show booths with accessories he would later return to Home Depot after use. Back then he was a trade show fiend, learning to sweet-talk executives and sell his passion on the floors of conference centers from San Diego to Salt Lake City. His big break: REI. Woodman spent months messaging executives and shooting over progress reports before the outdoor sports giant succumbed, giving the company (which is still technically called Woodman Labs) a huge dose of validation.

With 2007 revenue in the low seven figures, Woodman had a crisis of confidence. GoPro's founder worried that he "couldn't take the company any further" and agreed to turn over majority control to a group of outside investors. And that deal likely would have gone down except for the 2008 financial crisis. The investors wanted to lower the valuation, and Woodman, his pride hurt and his spine stiffened, refused. "We were going up and to the right, and the economy wasn't even affecting GoPro," he said. The company wound up exceeding $8 million in sales that year and has continued its organic growth. The next turning point came in 2010 when Best Buy began carrying GoPro. Woodman's little idea had gone mainstream.

A LITTLE MORE THAN seventy-two hours after the ski trip to Big Sky country, a handful from GoPro's team and I were half a mile off the coast of Half Moon Bay, California, in a watercraft normally reserved for Navy Seals. Two hundred yards away, the world's best surfers hurtled down the famed Mavericks surf break armed only with longboards, hubris, and—yes, GoPros.

From our vessel, part of a forty-watercraft flotilla of paddleboards, pleasure craft, and dinghies, we watched 35-foot waves crash and clatter, mixing sea spray with diesel fumes. Woodman tested the first GoPro prototypes near these same icy waters. Looking around, the cameras were ubiquitous, dangling from the mouths of surfers, held up by spectators and strapped to the helmets of Jet Ski–zipping water rescuers. "You gotta GoPro the GoPro boat," yelled out one onlooker from her craft, proceeding to point her gray box toward our vessel. Hours later, footage of our boat and the day's surfers ended up on YouTube.

Indeed, social media friendliness explains how GoPro went from niche to blockbuster. In the hands of the right athletes, the footage shot on a point-of-view action camera is viral crack. For weekend warriors, it's the easiest way to get your own three minutes of glory.

Though Woodman personally lacks a Twitter account and is inactive on Facebook, he spends millions of dollars a year to make sure the GoPro name is hashtagged with that blood-pumping shot of the GoPro-backed Shaun White pulling off a 1080, or Felix Baumgartner plunging toward the ground from the upper echelons of Earth's atmosphere (Baumgartner wore five GoPros on his record-breaking jump). "We're building one of the world's most engaging and exciting consumer brands, and it's largely on the content that our customers are creating with their GoPros," Woodman said. GoPro boasts about 500 million views on its YouTube channel and 7.5 million likes on Facebook.

"It's funny to see so many people with them, but it makes sense and that's great for the brand," said surfer Kelly Slater, one of the many GoPro-sponsored athletes. "They've quickly monopolized the idea in a way Band-Aid or Q-tip has where everyone refers to these types of shots as GoPro shots or expect they must've been shot with one."

GoPro's competitors are the first to acknowledge this. Giovanni Tomaselli, founder of action camera maker iON Worldwide, said Woodman "deserves to be a billionaire" for his innovation and that iON had "taken a leaf out of [GoPro's] book" when it came to promoting its first products, which launched in 2012. But he remained defiant: "We do not believe this category is one-size-fits-all."

There are also those who believe the category may not be here to stay. While smartphones killed the need to own camcorders like the ill-fated Flip Video camera, they may also have the capacity to one day become the device that takes out GoPro. Valley venture capitalist Greg Gretsch called GoPro an "ephemeral opportunity."

"The issue is that they're a hardware manufacturer in a world that's quickly moving to the überplatform: the smartphone," he added, pointing out that iPhone and Android operating systems have hundreds of developers writing software every day.

Meanwhile, GoPro must now deal with the big boys, who have finally taken note of his success. Sony shipped its first action cameras in 2012 and is positioning itself as a "strong number two" with features like image stabilization and stereo sound, which GoPro currently lacks. "We're a camera company first," said Sony product manager Greg Herd. "GoPro is a mount company first that sourced to cameras."

Woodman said that the market he created is big enough for multiple companies. And he was only too happy to point out the stat about outselling Sony at Best Buy in December 2012. "For the first time Sony got beat, and it was GoPro?" Woodman asks rhetorically. "That's pretty awesome."

Nonetheless, he's also smart enough to know that GoPro needs to step up its game. That explains the Foxconn deal, which brought in a key strategic partner, and the IPO, which allowed GoPro to tap into Wall Street. "Would being a public company put us in a better position to compete?" Woodman asked rhetorically. "We'll see."

TWO MONTHS AFTER CLOSING the Foxconn deal, Woodman tried to say the word "awesome" again, but in an open cockpit at 2,000 feet, it's a little hard to talk. Soaring above the vineyards of California's Sonoma County in a World War II–era biplane, GoPro's founder flapped his arms in sheer bliss. He took the pilot's barrel roll to little ill effect and saluted a stomach-knotting midair stall known as a hammerhead with his trademark yell, "YEEEEEEEEEEEEEEEOW," which was quickly swallowed by the sound of the plane's propeller.

Having conquered the slopes and the sea, Woodman now wanted to make GoPro the go-to device for capturing "life's precious moments." He's not the only who thinks that.

"My vision is to help global consumers build an ecosystem in which capturing, sharing, viewing, and creating content on any device at any time in any place is convenient, effortless, and cost-effective," says Foxconn CEO Terry Gou. "GoPro fits well into that ecosystem."

That's a big leap. But GoPro's trajectory still remains up and to the right, and will continue that way as long as it finds new uses and markets for its cameras. "If we can become the de facto standard for image capture of unique perspectives around the world, we have a lot of growth ahead of us," Woodman said. Capturing some of those unique perspectives were the eight GoPros trained on the CEO as he exited the biplane. As he unbuckled himself from his harness and hopped out of the plane, the cameras caught some of his first words once he was back on the ground: "This does not suck."

CHAPTER 10

Brian Chesky, Airbnb:
The Sharing Economy's Broker

While the classic path to Internet riches holds that you should blow up an industry, Brian Chesky, thirty-two, has built a billion-dollar personal fortune for himself and two partners by creating an entirely new one. His company, Airbnb, is a clearinghouse that matches people who have extra space in their home with visitors looking for a place to crash, the most advanced example of the new, multibillion-dollar peer-to-peer "sharing" economy. There may be no truer Web 2.0 company, existing entirely on the shoulders of earlier Internet innovations: feedback rating systems, which provide crowdsourced seals of approval for both sides of a transaction; social media, which can be used to verify identities and conduct background checks; and smartphones, which allow us all to become stores, wherever we are. As **Tomio Geron** discovered in 2013, this phenomenon is far bigger that Chesky realized when he made some easy money letting designers crash on his floor, and it's not going anywhere, as Airbnb's recent $10 billion valuation demonstrated.

———

On paper, Frederic Larson is just one data point in five years of U.S. government statistics showing underemployment in dozens of industries and stagnant income growth across the board. The sixty-three-year-old photographer with two children in college was downsized by the *San Francisco Chronicle* in 2009. He now spends his time teaching at Academy of Art University, with occasional lecturing gigs in Hawaii. A far cry from the salary, benefits, and company car he used to have.

But Larson is also a data point in an economic revolution that is quietly turning millions of people into part-time entrepreneurs, and disrupting old notions about consumption and ownership. Twelve days per month Larson rents his Marin County home on website Airbnb for $100 a night, of which he nets $97. Four nights a week he transforms his Prius into a de facto taxi via the ride-sharing service Lyft, pocketing another $100 a night in the process.

It isn't glamorous—on nights that he rents out his house, he removes himself to one room that he's cordoned off, and he showers at the gym—but in leveraging his hard assets into seamless income streams, he's generating $3,000 a month. "I've got a product, which is what I share: my Prius and my house," said Larson. "Those are my two sources of income."

Welcome to the *sharing economy,* where asset owners use digital clearinghouses to capitalize on the unused capacity of things they already have, and consumers rent from their peers rather than rent or

buy from a company. Airbnb is the poster child for this phenomenon, sprinting ahead of one-hundred-plus companies which have
sprouted up over the past five years, offering owners a tiny income
stream out of dozens of types of physical assets that would never before have been considered monetizable. A few dozen square feet in a
driveway can now produce income via Parking Panda. A pooch-
friendly room in your house is suddenly a pet penthouse via DogVa-
cay. On Liquid, for $20 a day an unused bicycle becomes a way for
a traveler to cheaply get around while visiting town.

"People providing these services in many ways are entrepreneurs or
micro-entrepreneurs," said Airbnb cofounder Brian Chesky. "They're
more independent, more liberated, a little more economically empow-
ered."

With an estimated $250 million in revenue in 2013, generated
mostly from commissions on all this dealing, Chesky's company is
singlehandedly funneling billions of dollars into people's wallets
(one study estimates that in New York City alone, it generates $650
million in economic activity) creating an income boost in a stagnant
wage market—and a disruptive economic force.

And it's not just a bicoastal thing. Chesky is quick to point to
one heartland town, where his company has three hosts willing to
rent their place for as low as $40 a night.

Peoria.

THE GENESIS OF THE modern-day sharing economy can be traced to
San Francisco in 2008, where Chesky and Joe Gebbia, recent Rhode
Island School of Design graduates who had fled west, thought they
could make some pocket cash by housing attendees at an industrial

design conference on air beds in their apartment. They put up a site, Airbedandbreakfast.com, to advertise their floor space. After three people bunked with them that week, they decided to max out their credit cards and build a bigger site with more listings. "We never considered the notion we were participating in a new economy," said Chesky. "We were just trying to solve our own problem. After we solved our own problem, we realized many other people want this."

To beef up their tech chops the two designers brought in Nathan Blecharczyk, Gebbia's former roommate. Early on, the trio focused their site—rechristened Airbnb—on large events where hotels were sold out, such as the 2008 Democratic and Republican conventions. In 2009 they got into the hot Silicon Valley accelerator Y Combinator, yet cofounder Paul Graham was dubious. The Airbnb partners impressed him with wacky gambits like "Obama O's" and "Captain McCain" breakfast cereals, which they first gave away to bloggers to get publicity, then ended up selling for $40 a box to support the company. "We were skeptical about the idea but loved the founders," said Graham. Chesky and crew then won over Sequoia Capital, which came up with $600,000 in seed funding.

Airbnb started slowly, facing the critical mass problem that all marketplaces do—buyers want more sellers and vice versa. There was also a social stigma around sharing. A lot of people told Chesky that renting to strangers was a "weird thing, a crazy idea." To attract more hosts the Airbnb founders went to New York in 2009, where many of its users lived, to meet them personally—the opposite of what an Internet company typically does—and learn how to improve.

Newspapers brokered the swapping of assets for a century. Various Internet innovations have allowed Airbnb, and its ilk, to exponentially improve the opportunity. Ebay's much duplicated rating system bestows commercial credibility on individuals. With Facebook you can go further, checking people's profiles before renting to them. Smartphone apps let sharers transact anywhere, see what's being shared nearby, and pay on the spot.

Airbnb has a broker's model. In exchange for providing the market and services like customer support, payment handling, and $1 million in insurance for hosts, Airbnb takes a 3 percent cut from the renter and a 6 percent to 12 percent cut from the traveler, depending on the property price.

In 2009, Airbnb ended with 100,000 guest nights booked, but growth started to tick up faster after adding features like escrow payments and professional photography services, and allowing different kinds of spaces such as whole houses, driveways, and even castles and tree houses. By 2010 the site had gone international and guest nights booked rose to 750,000. By 2011 it passed 2 million total nights booked. And by 2012, that figured approached 15 million. Critical mass had been achieved. On New Year's Eve that year, 141,000 people worldwide stayed at an Airbnb. In single-occupancy terms, that's almost 50 percent more than can fit in all the rooms in all the hotels on the Las Vegas Strip.

Those figures still pale next to the entire U.S. hotel industry, which sells more than 1 billion nights a year. But if you add Airbnb's 600,000 listings to the equivalent type of places available on vacation-oriented sites like HomeAway, suddenly house-sharing is larger in terms of room count than all the Hilton-branded hotels in the world. Wedbush Securities analyst Michael Pachter believes that Airbnb will eventually get to 100 million nights per year.

Chesky and his crew have the war chest to go for it. In 2011, Airbnb raised $112 million from the likes of Sequoia, Greylock

Partners, and Andreessen Horowitz, at a valuation of $1.3 billion. "The potential is huge," said Sequoia's Greg McAdoo. "In 20 years we won't be able to imagine a world where we didn't have access to things through collaborative consumption."

Then in 2014 came the whopper: a $400 million round, valuing the company at $10 billion. On paper, Chesky, Gebbia, and Blecharczyk have now all joined the billionaires club. And their company has yet to turn a profit.

AIRBNB HAD GREAT TIMING and fast-moving founders but benefited equally from a sea change over the past five years in consumer attitudes about ownership, a shift that could prove to be the longest-lasting legacy of the Great Recession.

The lesson learned was basic and deeply ingrained: Borrowing to buy assets above your means is a sketchy proposition, as 16.5 million foreclosed houses attest. Ownership, the root of the American Dream, took a hit. "It's changed, especially with the younger generation," said Shannon King, chair for strategic planning at the National Association of Realtors. "Also they like the idea of not being tied into a property. They can move to different areas of town and live a more flexible lifestyle."

And that new paradigm trickled down far past real estate. With cars, for example, the old ideal of buying a ride after high school to squire friends and dates is eroding. The share of new cars bought by Americans eighteen to thirty-four dropped from 16 percent in 2007 to 12 percent in 2012, according to Edmunds.com.

Millennials, the ascendant economic force in America, have been culturally programmed to borrow, rent, and share. They don't buy newspapers; they grab and disseminate stories à la carte via Facebook and Twitter. They don't buy DVD sets; they stream shows. They don't buy CDs; they subscribe to music on services such as Spotify or Pandora (or just steal it). Sabrina Hernandez, twenty-three, used to work at Starbucks, but she isn't going back after averaging $1,200 a month this fall hosting strangers' dogs in her apartment through website DogVacay. "It's so much more rewarding than working in a customer-service setting."

Old industries are scrambling to adjust. While hotels so far are letting regulators do the dirty work of targeting Airbnb—from occupancy taxes to insurance to apartment building bylaws, the sharing economy presents a raft of sticky issues—the auto industry is pivoting. Besides the Avis acquisition of Zipcar, Mercedes-owner Daimler has been rapidly expanding its car2go sharing service that rents its Smart Fortwo cars by the minute. And General Motors invested in a $3 million round in RelayRides. The reason? Marketing. GM hopes people sharing a Chevy will eventually buy one. Additionally, GM can incentivize sales by promoting the idea that a new car can now come with a rental income stream attached. You can even open your GM car with RelayRides' iPhone app using GM's OnStar system.

Economists remain perplexed as to how to measure all this activity. "We're going to have to invent new economics to capture the impact of the sharing economy," said Arun Sundararajan, a professor at the Stern School of Business at NYU, who studies this phenomenon. The largest question for academics is whether this all creates new value or just replaces existing businesses.

The answer is surely both. It's classic creative destruction. There may be a short-term negative for the economy because a person isn't buying a car. But long-term economic efficiencies result, and that's ultimately good for everyone. Chesky's Airbnb commissioned a study of its economic impact on San Francisco and found a "spill-over effect." Because an Airbnb rental tends to be cheaper than a hotel, people stay longer and spent $1,100 in the city, compared with $840 for hotel guests; 14 percent of their customers said they would not have visited the city at all without Airbnb.

"It's never been the case in our economy that utilizing assets more efficiently leads to fewer jobs," said Robert Atkinson, president of the Information Technology and Innovation Foundation. "If I were in hotels, I wouldn't lose a lot of sleep over it."

And perhaps it's even artificial to divide the world into the individual versus the corporation. Many critics deride Airbnb and the like as short-term fads for slow economic times. (Airbnb's report found that 42 percent of hosts use the income to pay everyday living expenses.) Safety, value, customer service, and quality of goods remain areas where it could stumble.

But human beings have been swapping before money even existed. New technologies only grease the wheels of these ancient transactional instincts. Even if growth levels off, it doesn't change the fact that peer exchanges like Airbnb are simply another way for entrepreneurs to reach customers.

CHAPTER 11

Alex Karp, Palantir: Meet Big Brother

There's virtually no company in the world—certainly in the transparency-will-save-us tech world—as mysterious as Palantir. Few people understand what it does, or the extent to which its data-mining systems and custom-built programs and techniques can perform impossibly complex tasks with the push of a button. As a force for good, it can track terrorists for the government and detect fraud and hacking for corporations. The omniscience Palantir empowers (and the CIA money that first funded it), however, has many a civil libertarian describing it in Orwellian terms.

If Big Brother has a human face, it's Alex Karp. A self-described "deviant" philosopher, he found himself, at first by chance (he was the favored law school intellectual sparring partner of Palantir cofounder Peter Thiel) and then by instinct, running a company with powers previously reserved for all-knowing gods. **Andy Greenberg** and **Ryan Mac** were the first to introduce Karp, now forty-seven, and Palantir to the wider world, and they did so at a critical time: Palantir, at the tail end of 2013, was raising big money at big valuations (enough to almost make Karp a billionaire) and looking to expand its reach in the private sector. In the world of WikiLeaks and Snowden, it's a tale that can affect us all.

———

Ever since rumors spread that a startup called Palantir helped to kill Osama bin Laden, Alex Karp hasn't had much time to himself. On one sunbaked morning in the summer of 2013, Palantir's lean chief executive, who sports a top-heavy mop of frazzled hair, hiked the grassy hills around Stanford University's massive satellite antennae known as the Dish, a favorite meditative pastime. But his solitude was disturbed somewhat by "Mike," an ex-Marine—silent, six foot one, 270 pounds of mostly pectoral muscle—who trails him everywhere he goes. Even on the suburban streets of Palo Alto, steps from Palantir's headquarters, the bodyguard lingered a few feet behind.

"It puts a massive cramp on your life," Karp complained, his expression hidden behind large black sunglasses. "There's nothing worse for reducing your ability to flirt with someone."

Karp's 24/7 security detail is meant to protect him from extremists who have sent him death threats and conspiracy theorists who have called Palantir to rant about the Illuminati. Schizophrenics have stalked Karp outside his office for days at a stretch. "It's easy to be the focal point of fantasies," he said, "if your company is involved in realities like ours."

Palantir lives the realities of its customers: the NSA, the FBI, and the CIA—an early investor through its In-Q-Tel venture fund—along with an alphabet soup of other U.S. counterterrorism and military agencies. In the past six years, Palantir has become the go-to company for mining massive data sets for intelligence and law enforcement applications, with a slick software interface and coders who parachute into clients' headquarters to customize its programs. Palantir turns messy swamps of information into intuitively visualized maps, histograms, and link charts. Give its so-called forward-deployed engineers a few days to crawl, tag, and integrate every scrap of a customer's data, and Palantir can elucidate problems as disparate as terrorism, disaster response, and human trafficking.

Palantir's advisors include Condoleezza Rice and former CIA director George Tenet, who said in an interview that "I wish we had a tool of its power" before 9/11. General David Petraeus, the former CIA chief, described Palantir to *Forbes* as "a better mousetrap when a better mousetrap was needed" and calls Karp "sheer brilliant."

Among those using Palantir to connect the dots are the Marines, who have deployed its tools in Afghanistan for forensic analysis of roadside bombs and predicting insurgent attacks. The software helped locate Mexican drug cartel members who murdered an American customs agent, and tracked down hackers who installed spyware on the Dalai Lama's computer. In the book *The Finish*, detailing the killing of Osama bin Laden, author Mark Bowden writes that Palantir's software "actually deserves the popular designation Killer App."

Palantir has emerged from the shadow world of spies and special ops to take corporate America by storm. The same tools that can predict ambushes in Iraq are helping pharmaceutical firms analyze drug data. According to a former JPMorgan Chase staffer, they've saved the firm hundreds of millions of dollars by addressing issues from cyberfraud to distressed mortgages. A Palantir user visiting a bank can, in seconds, see connections between a Nigerian Internet protocol address, a proxy server somewhere within the U.S., and payments flowing out from a hijacked home equity line of credit, just as military customers piece together fingerprints on artillery shell fragments, location data, anonymous tips, and social media to track down Afghani bomb makers.

Those tools have allowed Palantir's T-shirted twentysomethings to woo customers away from the suits and ties of IBM, Booz Allen, and Lockheed Martin, with a product that deploys faster, offers cleaner results, and often costs less than $1 million per installation— a fraction of the price its rivals can offer. Its commercial clients— whose identities it guards even more closely than those of its government customers—include Bank of America and News Corp. Private sector deals now account for close to 60 percent of the company's revenue, which *Forbes* estimated hit more than $450 million in 2013, up from less than $300 million a year earlier. Karp projects Palantir will sign $1 billion in new, long-term contracts in 2014, a year that may also bring the company its first profits.

The bottom line: A CIA-funded firm run by an eccentric philosopher has become one of the most valuable private companies in tech, worth $9 billion, according to a round of funding in December 2013. Karp owns roughly a tenth of the firm—just less than its largest stakeholder, Peter Thiel, the PayPal and Facebook billionaire. (Other billionaire investors include Home Depot cofounder Ken Langone and hedge fund titan Stanley Druckenmiller.) If and when the company goes public, a possibility Karp says Palantir is reluctantly considering, his net worth will likely surge past $1 billion.

The biggest problem for Palantir's business may be just how well its software works: It helps its customers see too much. In the wake of NSA leaker Edward Snowden's revelations of the agency's mass surveillance, Palantir's tools have come to represent privacy advocates' greatest fears of data-mining technology—Google-level engineering applied directly to government spying. That combination of Big Brother and Big Data came into focus just as Palantir emerged as one of the fastest-growing startups in the Valley, threatening to contaminate its first public impressions and render the firm toxic in the eyes of customers and investors just when it needs them most.

"They're in a scary business," said Electronic Frontier Foundation attorney Lee Tien. ACLU analyst Jay Stanley has written that Palantir's software could enable a "true totalitarian nightmare, monitoring the activities of innocent Americans on a mass scale." Karp, a social theory PhD, doesn't dodge those concerns. He sees Palantir as the company that can rewrite the rules of the zero-sum game of privacy and security. "I didn't sign up for the government to know when I smoke a joint or have an affair," he acknowledged. In a company address he stated, "We have to find places that we protect away from government so that we can all be the unique and interesting and, in my case, somewhat deviant people we'd like to be."

Palantir boasts of technical safeguards for privacy that go well beyond the legal requirements for most of its customers, as well as a team of "privacy and civil liberties engineers." But it's Karp himself who ultimately decides the company's path. "He's our conscience," said senior engineer Ari Gesher.

The question looms, however, of whether business realities and competition will corrupt those warm and fuzzy ideals. When it comes to talking about industry rivals, Karp often sounds less like

Palantir's conscience than its id. He expressed his primary motivation in a 2013 company address: to "kill or maim" competitors like IBM and Booz Allen. "I think of it like survival," he said. "We beat the lame competition before they kill us."

KARP SEEMS TO ENJOY listing reasons he isn't qualified for his job. "He doesn't have a technical degree, he doesn't have any cultural affiliation with the government or commercial areas, his parents are hippies," he said, manically pacing around his office as he describes himself in the third person. "How could it be the case that this person is cofounder and CEO since 2005 and the company still exists?"

The answer dates back to Karp's decades-long friendship with Peter Thiel, starting at Stanford Law School. The two both lived in the no-frills Crothers dorm and shared most of their classes during their first year, but held starkly opposite political views. Karp had grown up in Philadelphia, the son of an artist and a pediatrician who spent many of their weekends taking him to protests for labor rights and against "anything Reagan did," he recalled. Thiel had already founded the staunchly libertarian *Stanford Review* during his time at the university as an undergrad.

"We would run into each other and go at it . . . like wild animals on the same path," Karp said. "Basically I loved sparring with him."

With no desire to practice law, Karp went on to study under Jürgen Habermas, one of the twentieth century's most prominent philosophers, at the University of Frankfurt. Not long after obtaining his doctorate, he received an inheritance from his grandfather, and began investing it in startups and stocks with surprising success. Some high-net-worth individuals heard that "this crazy dude was good at investing" and began to seek his services. To manage their money he set up the London-based Caedmon Group, a reference to Karp's middle name, the same as the first known English-language poet.

Back in Silicon Valley, Thiel had cofounded PayPal with Elon Musk, among others, and had sold it to eBay in October 2002 for $1.5 billion. He had gone on to create a hedge fund called Clarium Capital but continued to found new companies: One would become Palantir, named by Thiel for the *palantiri*, seeing stones, from J.R.R. Tolkien's Lord of the Rings, orbs that allow the holder to gaze across vast distances to track friends and foes.

In a post–9/11 world Thiel wanted to sell those *palantiri*-like powers to the growing national security complex: His concept for Palantir was to use the fraud-recognition software designed for Pay-Pal to stop terrorist attacks. But from the beginning the libertarian saw Palantir as an antidote to—not a tool for—privacy violations in a society slipping into a vise of security. "It was a mission-oriented company," said Thiel, who has personally invested $40 million in Palantir and today serves as its chairman. "I defined the problem as needing to reduce terrorism while preserving civil liberties."

In 2004, Thiel teamed up with Joe Lonsdale and Stephen Cohen, two Stanford computer science grads, and PayPal engineer Nathan Gettings to code together a rough product. Initially they were bankrolled entirely by Thiel, and the young team struggled to get investors or potential customers to take them seriously. "How the hell do you get them to listen to twenty-two-year-olds?" said Lonsdale. "We wanted someone to have a little more gray hair."

Enter Karp, whose Krameresque brown curls, European wealth connections, and PhD masked his business inexperience. Despite his nonexistent tech background, the founders were struck by his ability to immediately grasp complex problems and translate them to non-engineers.

Lonsdale and Cohen quickly asked him to become acting CEO, and as they interviewed other candidates for the permanent job, none of the starched-collar Washington types or MBAs they met impressed them. "They were asking questions about our diagnostic of the total available market," says Karp, disdaining the B-school lingo. "We were talking about building the most important company in the world."

While Karp attracted some early European angel investors, American venture capitalists seemed allergic to the company. According to Karp, Sequoia Chairman Michael Moritz doodled through an entire meeting. A Kleiner Perkins exec lectured the Palantir founders on the inevitable failure of their company for an hour and a half.

Palantir was rescued by a referral to In-Q-Tel, the CIA's venture arm, which would make two rounds of investment totaling more than $2 million. "They were clearly top-tier talent," said former In-Q-Tel executive Harsh Patel. "The most impressive thing about the team was how focused they were on the problem . . . how humans would talk with data."

That mission turned out to be vastly more difficult than any of the founders had imagined. PayPal had started with perfectly structured and organized information for its fraud analysis. Intelligence customers, by contrast, had mismatched collections of e-mails, recordings, and spreadsheets.

To fulfill its privacy and security promises, Palantir needed to catalog and tag customers' data to ensure that only users with the right credentials could access it. This need-to-know system meant classified information couldn't be seen by those without proper clearances—and was also designed to prevent the misuse of sensitive personal data.

But Palantir's central privacy and security protection would be what Karp terms, with his academic's love of jargon, "the immutable log." Everything a user does in Palantir creates a trail that can be audited. No Russian spy, jealous husband, or Edward Snowden can use the tool's abilities without leaving an indelible record of his or her actions.

From 2005 to 2008, the CIA was Palantir's patron and only customer, alpha-testing and evaluating its software. But with Langley's imprimatur, word of Palantir's growing abilities spread, and the motley Californians began to bring in deals and recruits. The philosopher Karp turned out to have a unique ability to recognize and seduce star engineers. His colleagues were so flummoxed by his nose for technical talent that they once sent a pair of underwhelming applicants into a final interview with Karp as a test. He smelled both out immediately.

A unique Palantir culture began to form in Karp's iconoclast image. Its Palo Alto headquarters, which it calls "the Shire" in reference to the homeland of Tolkien's hobbits, features a conference room turned giant plastic ball pit and has floors littered with Nerf darts and dog hair. (Canines are welcome.) Staffers, most of whom choose to wear Palantir-branded apparel daily, spend so much time at the office that some leave their toothbrushes by the bathroom sinks.

Karp himself remains the most eccentric of Palantir's eccentrics. The lifelong bachelor, who says that the notion of settling down and raising a family gives him "hives," is known for his obsessive personality: He solves Rubik's cubes in less than three minutes, swims and practices the meditative art of Qigong daily, and has gone through aikido and jujitsu phases that involved putting cofounders in holds in the Shire's hallways. A cabinet in his office is stocked with vitamins, twenty pairs of identical swimming goggles, and hand sanitizer. He addresses his staff using an internal video channel called KarpTube, speaking on wide-ranging subjects like greed, integrity, and Marxism. "The only time I'm not thinking about Palantir," he said, "is when I'm swimming, practicing Qigong, or during sexual activity."

In 2010, Palantir's customers at the New York Police Department referred the company to JPMorgan, which would become its first commercial customer. A team of engineers rented a Tribeca loft, sleeping in bunk beds and working around the clock to help untangle the bank's fraud problems. Soon they were given the task of unwinding its toxic mortgage portfolio. Today Palantir's New York operation has expanded to a full, Batman-themed office known as Gotham, and its lucrative financial-services practice includes everything from predicting foreclosures to battling Chinese hackers.

As its customer base grew, however, cracks began to show in Palantir's idealistic culture. In early 2011 e-mails emerged that showed a Palantir engineer had collaborated on a proposal to deal with a WikiLeaks threat to spill documents from Bank of America. The Palantir staffer had eagerly agreed in the e-mails to propose tracking and identifying the group's donors, launching cyberattacks on WikiLeaks' infrastructure and even threatening its sympathizers. When the scandal broke, Karp put the offending engineer on leave and issued a statement personally apologizing and pledging the company's support for "progressive values and causes." Outside counsel was retained to review the firm's actions and policies and, after some deliberation, determined it was acceptable to rehire the offending employee, much to the scorn of the company's critics.

Following the WikiLeaks incident, Palantir's privacy and civil liberties team created an ethics hotline for engineers called the Batphone: Any engineer can use it to anonymously report to Palantir's directors work on behalf of a customer they consider unethical. As the result of one Batphone communication, for instance, the company backed out of a job that involved analyzing information on public Facebook pages. Karp has also stated that Palantir turned down a chance to work with a tobacco firm, and overall the company says it walks away from as much as 20 percent of its possible revenue for ethical reasons. (It remains to be seen whether the company will be so picky if it becomes accountable to public shareholders and the demand for quarterly results.)

Still, according to former employees, Palantir has explored work in Saudi Arabia despite the staff's misgivings about human rights abuses in the kingdom. And for all Karp's emphasis on values, his apology for the WikiLeaks affair also doesn't seem to have left much of an impression in his memory. In an address to Palantir engineers in 2013, he sounded defiant: "We've never had a scandal that was really our fault."

AT 4:07 P.M. ON November 14, 2009, Michael Katz-Lacabe was parking his red Toyota Prius in the driveway of his home in the quiet Oakland suburb of San Leandro when a police car drove past. A license plate camera mounted on the squad car silently and routinely snapped a photo of the scene: his off-white, single-floor house, his wilted lawn and rosebushes, and his five- and eight-year-old daughters jumping out of the car.

Katz-Lacabe, a gray-bearded and shaggy-haired member of the local school board, community activist, and blogger, saw the photo only a year later: In 2010 he learned about the San Leandro Police Department's automatic license plate readers, designed to constantly photograph and track the movements of every car in the city. He filed a public records request for any images that included either of his two cars. The police sent back 112 photos. He found the one of his children most disturbing.

"Who knows how many other people's kids are captured in these images?" he asked. His concerns went beyond a mere sense of parental protection. "With this technology you can wind back the clock and see where everyone is, if they were parked at the house of someone other than their wife, a medical marijuana clinic, a Planned Parenthood center, a protest."

As Katz-Lacabe dug deeper, he found that the millions of pictures collected by San Leandro's license plate cameras are now passed on to the Northern California Regional Intelligence Center (NCRIC), one of seventy-two federally run intelligence fusion organizations set up after 9/11. That's where the photos are analyzed using software built by a company just across San Francisco Bay: Palantir.

In the business proposal that Palantir sent NCRIC, it offered customer references that included the Los Angeles and New York City police departments, boasting that it enabled searches of the NYPD's 500 million plate photos in less than five seconds. Katz-Lacabe contacted Palantir about his privacy concerns, and the company responded by inviting him to its headquarters for a sit-down meeting. When he arrived at the Shire, a pair of employees gave him an hour-long presentation on Palantir's vaunted safeguards: its access controls, immutable logs, and the Batphone.

Katz-Lacabe wasn't impressed. Palantir's software, he points out, has no default time limits—all information remains searchable for as long as it's stored on the customer's servers. And its auditing function? "I don't think it means a damn thing," he said. "Logs aren't useful unless someone is looking at them."

When Karp heard Katz-Lacabe's story, he quickly parried: Palantir's software saves lives. "Here's an actual use case," he said, launching into the story of a pedophile driving a "beat-up Cadillac" who was arrested within an hour of assaulting a child, thanks to NYPD license plate cameras. "Because of the license-plate-reader data they gathered in our product, they pulled him off the street and saved human children lives.

"If we as a democratic society believe that license plates in public trigger Fourth Amendment protections, our product can make sure you can't cross that line," he said, adding that there should be time limits on retaining such data. Until the law changes, though, Palantir will play within those rules. "In the real world where we work—which is never perfect—you have to have trade-offs."

And what if Palantir's audit logs—its central safeguard against abuse—are simply ignored? Karp responded that the logs are intended to be read by a third party. In the case of government agencies, he suggested an oversight body that reviews all surveillance—an institution that is purely theoretical at the moment. "Something like this will exist," Karp insisted. "Societies will build it, precisely because the alternative is letting terrorism happen or losing all our liberties."

Palantir's critics, unsurprisingly, weren't reassured by Karp's hypothetical court. Electronic Privacy Information Center activist Amie Stepanovich called Palantir "naïve" to expect the government to start policing its own use of technology. The Electronic Frontier

Foundation's Lee Tien derided Karp's argument that privacy safeguards can be added to surveillance systems after the fact. "You should think about what to do with the toxic waste while you're building the nuclear power plant," he argued, "not some day in the future."

Some former Palantir staffers said they felt equally concerned about the potential rights violations their work enabled. "You're building something that could absolutely be used for malice. It would have been a nightmare if J. Edgar Hoover had these capabilities in his crusade against Martin Luther King," said one former engineer. "One thing that really troubled me was the concern that something I contribute to could prevent an Arab Spring–style revolution."

Despite Palantir's lofty principles, said another former engineer, its day-to-day priorities are satisfying its police and intelligence customers: "Keeping good relations with law enforcement and 'keeping the lights on' bifurcate from the ideals."

He went on to argue that even Palantir's founders don't quite understand the *palantiri* in *The Lord of the Rings*. Tolkien's orbs, he pointed out, didn't actually give their holders honest insights. "The *palantiri* distort the truth," he said. And those who look into them, he added, "only see what they want to see."

DESPITE WHAT ANY CRITIC says, it's clear that Alex Karp does indeed value privacy—his own.

His office, decorated with cardboard effigies of himself built by Palantir staff and a Lego fortress on a coffee table, overlooks Palo Alto's Alma Street through two-way mirrors. Each pane is fitted with a wired device resembling a white hockey puck. The gadgets, known as acoustic transducers, imperceptibly vibrate the glass with white noise to prevent eavesdropping techniques, such as bouncing lasers off windows to listen to conversations inside.

He reminisced about a more carefree time in his life—years before Palantir, putting down his Rubik's cube to better gesticulate. "I had $40,000 in the bank, and no one knew who I was. I loved it. I loved it. I just loved it. I just loved it!" he said, his voice rising and his hands waving above his head. "I would walk around, go into skanky places in Berlin all night. I'd talk to whoever would talk to me, occasionally go home with people, as often as I could. I went to places where people were doing things, smoking things. I just loved it.

"One of the things I find really hard and view as a massive drag . . . is that I'm losing my ability to be completely anonymous."

It's not easy for a man in Karp's position to be a deviant in the modern world. And with tools like Palantir in the hands of the government, deviance may not be easy for the rest of us, either. With or without safeguards, the "complete anonymity" Karp savors may be a 20th-century luxury.

Karp lowers his arms, and the enthusiasm drains from his voice: "I have to get over this."

CHAPTER 12

Pejman Nozad, Angel Investor: Silicon Valley's Cinderella

While Pejman Nozad is the least successful subject of this book, as measured strictly by financial success or companies directly created, he's also among the most inspiring. Nozad isn't an entrepreneur full of disruptive ideas. He's not even the guy betting on the entrepreneur with the disruptive ideas. Instead, he's a person in the right location, at the right time in history, to put those camps together in a manner that is, in itself, earnestly brilliant. Silicon Valley is a meritocracy, where idea and execution rule over all else. But it still matters whom you know. And if you didn't go to Stanford, then perhaps the best place to get a deal to flow is a few miles down from campus, at the Medallion Rug Gallery.

Nozad, an Iranian immigrant, came into the tech game through selling carpets. That's it. Mix in charm, hustle, smarts, and instinct, and you get a $100 million fortune. **Victoria Barret** found Nozad the way great reporters do—following the connection from one story to another (in this case, Drop-box's Drew Houston, who within days of meeting Nozad, reports that "basically, he was our pimp.") It's not often that a business saga reads like Cinderella. This one fits the slipper.

———

On a balmy February evening in Palo Alto, Pejman Nozad sipped tea on the deck of the Rosewood Hotel, the hot spot of venture capital's capital, Sand Hill Road. He chose a table situated just central enough so that he could see everyone who walked in. As usual, it was packed with the startup crowd—entrepreneurs in thick-rimmed glasses and jeans mingling with their backers, finance types in pressed slacks and camel-colored Italian leather loafers. Nozad has the peppered-hair look of one of the money guys, but in his soft blue blazer, adorned with a pastel paisley pocket square, he buoyantly bridged both groups.

"There's Mike Abbott. You know him? One of the smartest guys I know, just brilliant," said Nozad, waving him over for a warm hello. He asked about his kids. Abbott had just left Twitter, where he ran engineering, for a partner spot at venture shop Kleiner Perkins Caufield & Byers. As Abbott left, Nozad leapt up. "My gosh, how are you?" he said, motioning over Lorenzo Thione, the Italian-born cofounder of search firm Powerset (which sold to Microsoft for $100 million in 2008). "I knew you wouldn't last at Microsoft," said Nozad, an early investor in Powerset. "Starting things is in your DNA."

Thione beamed a wide smile as he describes his latest "passion," a Netflix-like service for high-end contemporary art. He mentioned how much money he was looking for. Nozad leaned in a little: "This is so fascinating. I have people you should talk to. I know the top interior designers in New York. And I want to meet your cofounder. I never invest without that."

As the patio cooled, Nozad scanned the bar. The Rosewood was morphing into the night. The tech set had scuttled their iPads, settling in for cocktails, as a few coiffed call girls worked the crowd—perhaps the surest sign yet that money again flows freely in techland. Nozad wanted the L-shaped couch just at the corner of the entrance. "I'm afraid my friends might not find me," he told a buxom waitress.

Ensconced in his new perch, he spotted Darian Shirazi, who joined Facebook out of high school as its first intern and early hire. Within minutes Nozad listed names of key investors and possible board members Shirazi should seek out for his business data startup, Radius. In the same breath Nozad mentioned a friend Shirazi should set up his cousin with. "He is the nicest guy, but she has to move from London," said Nozad emphatically. "She belongs here." Shirazi chimed in, acting as cultural translator: "Persians are always matchmaking."

And, yes, that's exactly what he's doing, all day of every day. Nozad is one of Silicon Valley's greatest connectors. Top investors take his calls. Hit-making entrepreneurs consider him an uncle. And somewhere in between he's piling up small stakes in some of the hottest startups in the world. Yet Nozad doesn't have the staple calling card of Silicon Valley. No MBA. No PhD. No "technical background whatsoever" (his words). He's never even worked at a technology company.

Nozad's path to Silicon Valley power broker—and VC investor

with a net worth in the ballpark of $100 million—was a far simpler one: He sold carpets.

UNIVERSITY AVENUE REFLECTS PALO Alto's diversity in full. It starts as an exit off the Dumbarton Bridge, which cuts across the southern edge of San Francisco Bay, runs though rough-and-tumble East Palo Alto, then tree-lined stretches dotted with multimillion-dollar mansions, and eventually hits, as the name implies, the Stanford campus. A few hundred feet before that terminus, across from a Starbucks and a Thai restaurant, sits the Medallion Rug Gallery, a warehouse-like store where for thirty-six years the Amidi family has been selling "exquisite art forms" that just happen to cover your floor.

In 1994 the family patriarch, Amir Amidi, found himself on the phone with Nozad, who despite no tangible experience and a poor command of English, had answered a television ad for a salesperson. "Have you ever sold anything?" Amidi asked the brash caller in Farsi.

"No, but give me a chance," Nozad responded. "How can you deny someone you haven't even met?"

Nozad had already learned that you can't get something if you don't ask. He grew up in Tehran, but in the 1980s his family fled to Germany. Nozad intended to join them after his compulsory stint in Iran's military service, which he would satisfy by playing soccer for the country's premier team. When a military officer questioned his discharge, on account of his sporty tour of duty, Nozad found a high-level cleric and published an interview with him on the benefits of soccer—and then had that cleric expedite his discharge.

Within a month of rejoining his family in Mannheim, Germany, with the intent of playing more soccer, his brother persuaded him to show up at the U.S. consulate and ask for a visa. It was a set-up of sorts. His brother was obsessed with American culture and went to the consulate almost daily only to be denied. Nozad showed up one morning, mentioned his soccer interviewing days and promptly scored a journalism visa. Two months after that he was on a plane to San Francisco, where an uncle lived, with $700 and a few words of English.

He worked at a car wash in San Jose owned by Iranians and then a coffee and yogurt shop in Redwood City tucked between a Mexican restaurant and a Social Security office. He studied English at night, living in a small room above the shop cluttered with boxes of napkins, cups, and coffee beans. That's when he stumbled upon the carpet want ad placed, fortuitously, by an older Iranian immigrant who had made a success of himself after fleeing his homeland when the Shah was deposed.

"My father had the experience, Pejman had the enthusiasm," said Amidi's son, Saeed (Amidi died in 2000). "The American dream works both ways. A lot of rich people have to share their knowledge and take risks with a young person. That's how they stay rich. It's familiar, too. Someone did the same for them years ago."

Over the next fifteen years, as his English and confidence improved, Nozad proved Amidi's top rug seller, moving $8 million worth of floor coverings in his best year. But far more than that, he was an opportunist in the greatest sense. This American neophyte recognized that fate had bequeathed him access to the most important people in the most important region of the most important industry during its most important era.

So he made sure not to blow chance's gift. Nozad insisted on meeting his clients at their homes, toting along twenty or so rugs ("that's two hours of talking, at least"). And before these visits he researched his hosts on Google, so that he could turn showing carpets into a two-way tutorial, peppering each ever so gently with questions about their careers, their tastes, their views on how the world works. It was awkward at first. But within months of the routine he had names to drop and technology trends to ponder. "The smart ones understood me," he said. "They got it. They'd invite me to their office."

Nozad started playing host. He gathered some top VCs regularly at the rug store for meet-and-greet cocktails with entrepreneurs. "People used to tease me for going there," said Sequoia Capital's veteran partner Doug Leone. "At five o'clock the rugs would go up and flat screens would come down. We were all immigrants . . . Italians like me, Iranians, Indians. I was very comfortable."

Nozad still didn't have any significant assets to speak of. But his boss, who had come to call Nozad his "third son," had taken notice of his matchmaking skills. Amidi had also caught the VC bug. The family had purchased a small office building down the road from the rug store and took note as one tenant, Google, which had a few employees, exploded. Another tenant, PayPal, also grew out of its space—this time Amidi invested. "We noticed everyone around us was making more money than we were," said Saeed Amidi. "We wanted to be part of the big game."

In 1999, the Amidis formally launched an investment fund, cutting in Nozad as the de facto deal scout. It started with $2 million. Nozad kicked in $200,000, almost everything he had, for a one-third stake. The firm's name, Amidzad, even blended the two family names. While their investments were relatively small stakes— $25,000 or $250,000, the kind of numbers that most VCs wouldn't bother with—Nozad's hustle invariably earned him what Accel Partners' Sameer Gandhi terms "the Pejman exception."

"He has a good sniffer, and I trust the guy," said Sequoia's Leone, who has let Nozad coinvest with him in four different companies. "He's like me, from the earth."

Nozad's first big bet was on a startup called Danger, which aimed to make handheld devices for exchanging data. Nozad had sold Danger's cofounder Andy Rubin a $5,000 rug. The deal took hours of negotiation, and Nozad was impressed. He inquired about Danger. He couldn't quite make sense of the technology, but after the first business meeting with Rubin (who now runs Google's Android division), Nozad turned to his mentor Amidi and said: "I would invest in that guy if he was selling red balloons. He will make things happen." And so Amidzad wrote a check for $400,000.

Danger became a mobile phone software firm and was acquired by Microsoft for $500 million, but by then Amidzad's stake had been diluted to a pittance. Nozad made just two times his investment over an eight-year stretch. Sam Ferdows was brought in as Amidzad's lawyer soon after the Danger deal. His memory: "Once a week Pejman was telling me about some new 'best deal ever.' He was doing business with handshakes. And no one ever read the fine print. I don't think they even realized there was fine print. Once, he told me a guy was going to give us a piece of his carried interest. What the heck does that mean?"

Nozad recognized his weakness and began doing deals only if someone more experienced, and whom he liked, was willing to put up funds, too. One of his first such helpers was Babak "Bobby" Yazdani, an early investor in Google and Salesforce.com. He advised Marc Benioff on his first key recruits and also founded Saba, a human resources software company. Nozad sold Yazdani a few rugs and then asked him to meet a chip designer with a startup idea. Why didn't Yazdani just blow him off politely? Yazdani explained: "There's a lot of humility in our culture. I'm talking about immigrants and entrepreneurs in Silicon Valley. We all had just our families and our educations when we came here. So when someone who you have a relationship with asks you to do something, you do it. It's a courtesy but also a discipline."

Yazdani has since invested in eight startups with Nozad. He's one hook that makes Nozad's money attractive. Joe Lonsdale already had one hit under his belt when he attended a dinner hosted by Nozad at a Persian restaurant. He had cofounded data-mining outfit Palantir and had many suitors knocking when he left to launch his second venture, a private wealth management technology service called Addepar. Nozad insisted Lonsdale meet with him and Yazdani. He delicately pushed the idea of meeting at Lonsdale's Los Altos house. "You learn a lot about someone in their home," said Nozad, in a nod to his carpet-peddling days. Then he watched how Lonsdale and Yazdani interacted. As for Lonsdale: "I like Pejman. I needed Bobby. He knows how to evolve a startup. I didn't know how to build a management structure over time."

Nozad sought out technology advisors, too. Lou Montulli, a founding engineer at Netscape, was one of his first Silicon Valley friends. In 1997, Montulli wandered into the rug store owning three rugs from "an ex-wife and an expensive decorator." He wanted to have them cleaned or, better yet, get rid of them. Nozad quickly had him buying two more rugs. He now has twenty in various homes. Nozad showed him antique looms and videos of weavers and walked him through the history of Iran's rug industry. "He made me appreciate the craft," said Montulli, who then brought in other Netscape millionaires in need of rugs. Over time they talked technology, and Nozad started introducing Montulli to entrepreneurs. "It seems like such a leap from rugs to startups. But he was seeing amazing deal flow. He built a great network, and that's one of the keys to doing this successfully," said Montulli.

Nozad's instincts weren't perfect—most notably, he walked away from a stake in Facebook and instead invested in Stanford's ill-fated version of a social network, Affinity Circles. ("Here is the e-mail from Sean Parker!" crowed Nozad as he pulls up a piece of would-be history on his iPhone.) But his track record overall was proving formidable, as many of his early investments were gobbled by the tech giants at prices five times what he put in, including Vudu, Vivu, Bix, and Milo. While far from wealthy, he was living a proper American dream.

And then he spotted two young entrepreneurs, Drew Houston and Arash Ferdowsi, at a Y Combinator conference in 2007, toting the demo of a cloud storage system they called Dropbox. He cornered Ferdowsi, chatting him up in Farsi, and within days had the pair visiting him at the rug shop.

Escorted to the back room for music and Persian tea, Houston was sure that it was all a joke. "I was waiting for the candid cameras to show up," he remembered.

But within a day Nozad had Dropbox pitching Sequoia for funds. He'd called his buddy Leone, who immediately e-mailed Houston for a meeting. "He was our biggest booster, and we'd met the guy that week," Houston added. Two days later Sequoia partner Mike Moritz (who said he "always takes Pejman's calls") dropped in early on Houston and Ferdowsi at their apartment to make the final decision. Two days after that Nozad delicately inserted himself into a wine-soaked dinner at Pane e Vino in San Francisco, where Sequoia partner Sameer Gandhi (who later went to Accel), Houston, and Ferdowsi hammered out a $1.2 million seed round.

Nozad barely said a word but made sure to leave that night with a piece in Dropbox for Amidzad. "He'd done the introduction, and we wanted to do right by him," says Gandhi. Based on Dropbox's 2014 raise, at a $9.6 billion valuation, that stake is worth in the ballpark of $150 million.

AS NOZAD WANDERED THROUGH a wood-paneled library at Stonebrook Court, a 30,000-square-foot Tudor mansion and estate owned by his buddy Kelly Porter in Los Altos Hills, just north of San Jose, he took note of the dreary nineteenth-century paintings covering the walls. A warm flame crackled in a carved marble fireplace. "Can you believe this exists here?" Nozad said. He peeked into the ballroom to admire the sixteenth-century painted Venetian ceiling. "I'm talking to Lady Gaga's people. I want to host a party here for all of my entrepreneurs. Wouldn't that be amazing?" he said. That wasn't totally absurd, as Nozad was an investor in the musician's startup, Backplane.

Porter works for a small mergers and acquisitions advisory firm. He was doing a favor of sorts for Nozad. Earlier in the day two dozen investment bankers and deal lawyers gathered in the ballroom of Stonebrook Court as the heads of corporate development from Google, Facebook, Twitter, and other top firms divulged where they were looking to do acquisitions. These are the kinds of cozy conversations that make Silicon Valley run. Nozad was invited, then asked to bring a few of his entrepreneurs, including a fresh-faced twenty-one-year-old who had just dropped out of Stanford to do something in social payments. The kid barely had a company.

During cocktails Nozad's scruffy-looking crew stuck together like a high school clique even though most barely know one another. Everyone else was wearing dark suits. "I still have to pinch myself every now and then," said Shane Hegde, the Stanford dropout. "That I'm here, living this life. Pejman is a great guide."

Nozad believes Hegde is "brilliant," and he invested in Swap, his nascent startup which hasn't gained traction. He didn't push introductions at the Stonebrook soiree, though. When an M&A lawyer asked Nozad what he does, he merely says he "invests in amazing people."

That business has gotten more complicated. It used to be a rich man's hobby. But a raft of so-called super angel funds, including Paul Graham's Y Combinator, Eric Schmidt's TomorrowVentures, and Ron Conway's SV Angel, have since raised hundreds of millions to dabble in newly launched startups, promising connections and expertise along with checks. "There are too many of them investing in too many deals," snickered one prominent venture capitalist. "This doesn't end well for a lot of white-haired guys who should know better." Meanwhile, the big-money venture capital firms are doing smaller deals to get early access into promising companies.

Nozad isn't worried. He can offer entrepreneurs something others won't. Once, he gave an entrepreneur his wife's Mitsubishi Mirage. The guy was twenty-one years old, had just moved from Israel, and was broke. A year later he had a stake in that same guy's startup, alongside Sequoia. In 2011, he invested in a guy's company to give him enough cash to move from Texas to Palo Alto. "I don't like his business idea, but he is brilliant," said Nozad. He regularly hosts events for Stanford's Persian student organization. The last one was a tour of Facebook's new headquarters. "They should hire all of these kids. They are so smart!" And one day, some of them will start companies and give Nozad a call.

A few nights later, Nozad gathered seven of his entrepreneurs in a private room at a New Orleans–style restaurant in Palo Alto. Three are Iranian. After a few glasses of wine the conversation drifted away from business models to stories of family back home. There were tales of nighttime caravans smuggling family members into the Afghan desert and talk about the years spent in limbo awaiting life in a better place. Nozad's eyes moistened as he described a trip he took to Iran a few years ago, bringing along his wife of nineteen years (his childhood sweetheart from Tehran) and his son and daughter.

He's come a long way from charming clerics into a military discharge. In 2010, Nozad decided to invest independently of Amidzad. He still does deals with the family but more are solo, where he is betting his own money. "I realized I'm actually kind of good at this," he said. "I wanted focus." He's already sitting on several windfalls besides Dropbox, including Addepar, the social networking site Path, social charity startup Causes, a gaming outfit, Badgeville, and dating site Zoosk. In 2013, he went further, opening a new venture firm with Mar Hershenson, a former entrepreneur with a doctorate in electrical engineering. They raised $40 million for the fund and have invested in start-ups like Sensor Tower, software to make targeted marketing easier, and Washio, a slick app that is the Uber of dry cleaning. The hustling middleman can now put serious money into his favorite deals.

And he still sells carpets—he's founded his own upscale rug gallery, bringing in his brother to run it. In America, where anything is still possible, such is how great fortunes apparently begin.

CHAPTER 13

Evan Spiegel, Snapchat:
The $3 Billion Bet

What do you call someone who is twenty-three, has a company with zero revenue, and turns down a $3 billion buyout from Mark Zuckerberg? Perhaps the brashest entrepreneur since . . . Zuckerberg. In rejecting Facebook's billions, Snapchat's Evan Spiegel made a decision that will be scrutinized for decades. It's revealing that Spiegel's age isn't what people snicker about—twenty is the new fifty, and his connection to the teen market, which has figured out the value of having their digital past disappear, Snapchat-style, drives the company's momentum.

People do, however, question his maturity, myself included. A fun backstory: When this *Forbes* cover story first appeared in early 2014, Spiegel took to Twitter to deny a key, cocky detail regarding Zuckerberg and revealed an e-mail exchange that seemed to back it up. But then the writer, **J.J. Colao**, produced an audiotape confirming

Spiegel's smack talk. And it turns out that the second half of the Zuckerberg e-mail, which Spiegel had conveniently clipped, also undermined his denial. So in one PR "master-stroke," he was able to tick off Zuck, *Forbes*, and a slew of already-skeptical tech industry observers. A speed bump on the road to glory? Or a telling anecdote en route to business infamy?

In December 2012, Facebook's Mark Zuckerberg, the richest twentysomething in history, reached out to Snapchat's Evan Spiegel, who oversees a revenue-less app that makes photos disappear, with an invitation, delivered to his personal e-mail account: Come to Menlo Park and let's get to know each other. Spiegel, who was then twenty-two, with more than a little in common with Zuckerberg, including his own legal battle against a college buddy who helped him start his company, wound up taking the meeting . . . on his turf.

Armed with the premise of meeting with architect Frank Gehry about designs for Facebook's headquarters, Zuckerberg flew to Spiegel's hometown, Los Angeles, arranging for a private apartment to host the secret sit-down. When Spiegel showed up with his co-founder Bobby Murphy, who serves as Snapchat's chief technology officer, Zuckerberg had a specific agenda ready. He tried to draw out the partners' vision for Snapchat—and he described Facebook's new product, Poke, a mobile app for sharing photos and making them disappear. It would debut in a matter of days. And in case any nuance could be missed, Zuckerberg would soon change the large sign outside Facebook's Silicon Valley campus from its iconic thumbs-up

"like" symbol to the Poke icon. Remembered Spiegel: "It was basically like, 'We're going to crush you.'"

Spiegel and Murphy immediately returned to their office and ordered a book for each of their six employees: Sun Tzu's *The Art
of War.*

Snapchat represents the greatest existential threat yet to the
Facebook juggernaut. Today's teens have finally learned the lesson
their older siblings failed to grasp: What you post on social media—
the good, the bad, the inappropriate—stays there forever. So they've
been signing up for Snapchat, with its *Mission: Impossible*–style det-
onation technology, in droves. *Forbes* estimated that, as of the beginning of 2014, 50 million people used Snapchat. Median age:
eighteen. Facebook, meanwhile, has admittedly seen a decline among
teenagers. Its average user is closer to forty.

Zuckerberg understood this, which might explain the games-
manship. When Poke debuted, on December 21, 2012, Zuckerberg
e-mailed Spiegel, telling him that he hoped he enjoyed it. Spiegel,
who had deactivated his Facebook account, frantically called Murphy for his review. It was, Murphy responded glumly, a near-exact
copy.

But a funny thing happened on the way to obsolescence. The
day after its launch, Poke hit number one on the iPhone App Store.
But within three days, on December 25, Snapchat had pulled ahead,
boosted by the publicity, as the Facebook app disappeared from the
top 30. Recalled Spiegel, with glee: "It was like, 'Merry Christmas,
Snapchat!'"

Which helps explain what happened in the fall of 2013 when Zuckerberg reengaged Spiegel, basically ready to surrender on terms so generous, on paper, they seemed preposterous: $3 billion in cash, according

to people familiar with the offer, for a two-year-old app with no revenue and no timetable for revenue. (Facebook refused to comment.)

Even more preposterous, of course: Spiegel turned Zuck down. It was the most scrutinized business decision of the past few years, complete with head-spinning math. *Forbes* estimated that Spiegel and Murphy each still owned about 25 percent of Snapchat at the time, which means they were both forgoing a $750 million windfall. "I can see why it's strategically valuable," said one leading venture capitalist. "But is it worth $3 billion? Not in any universe I'm aware of."

The roots of that decision, however, were obvious to anyone who knew about the primer that Spiegel and Murphy had bought for their team. Chapter 6 of *The Art of War* specifically addresses the need to attack an enemy where and when he displays weakness. Spiegel and Murphy sensed an opening and insisted that rather than selling, they're aiming to upend the social media hierarchy, armed with a $50 million war chest raised in December 2013 at a lower (but still heady) valuation of just under $2 billion. "There are very few people in the world who get to build a business like this," says Spiegel. "I think trading that for some short-term gain isn't very interesting."

For those keeping score, a "short-term gain" for a then-twenty-three-year-old who still lived in his dad's house now apparently equals three-quarters of a billion dollars. In going for the long gain, Spiegel will either become the next great billionaire prodigy or the ultimate cautionary tale of youthful hubris.

A LANKY SIX FOOT one, dressed in a button-down shirt, designer jeans, and plain white sneakers, Evan Spiegel hasn't molted the carapace of an awkward teen. As he sat in Snapchat's new Venice Beach headquarters for his first-ever in-depth media interview, he shifted abruptly from raucous laughter to icy glares, constantly grabbing fistfuls of gummy bears and Goldfish crackers. His conversation was pocked with plenty of examples of "like" and "whatever." And while Spiegel proved extremely opinionated on subjects like politics, music, and other techies, he was reluctant to discuss even the most basic CEO topics, like his ideal management team or his long-term vision for Snapchat.

If you're patient enough, however—one of the conversations with him lasted two and a half hours—you'll get the full backstory, one that shares an uncanny similarity to that of his frenemy, Zuckerberg.

Like Zuck, he was a child of relative privilege, the first-born child of two successful lawyers (mom Melissa went to Harvard Law and practiced tax law before Spiegel was born, while litigator dad John, a Yale Law grad, has represented the likes of Sergey Brin and Warner Bros.), living in tony Pacific Palisades, just east of Malibu. And like Zuck, he was a middle school nerd who found refuge in technology, building his first computer in sixth grade, experimenting with Photoshop in his school's computer lab and spending weekends at a local high school's art lab. "My best friend was the computer teacher, Dan," Spiegel laughed.

In high school he began to display the moxie that Zuckerberg would later exhibit, promoting Red Bull at clubs and bars and using his parents' divorce as a leverage tactic. He first moved in with his dad when he gave him a free hand in outfitting his room and who could come over. "I had some notorious parties," he smirked. But when Pop reportedly refused to shell out for the lease on a BMW 550i, he moved in with Mom. Days later the BMW was his. Except for college, he's been based in his dad's home, a stone-faced mansion a half-mile north of the ocean, ever since. "A lot of things have changed very quickly, so it's nice to have that one constant," he said by way of justification. "It's also pretty grounding."

He entered Stanford's product design program and in 2010, during his sophomore year, moved into the Kappa Sigma fraternity house. Bobby Murphy, a senior major in mathematics and computational science, lived across the hall. "We weren't cool," Murphy said of the fraternity. "So we tried to build things to be cool."

While Spiegel speaks animatedly, albeit measuring what he's saying, Murphy, the Berkeley son of state employees (his mother emigrated from the Philippines), sits placidly, one leg tucked under the other. "I'd describe him almost like a monk," said David Kravitz, Snapchat's first hire. "I don't think I've ever seen him upset." At Stanford it was Murphy who first hired Spiegel, recruiting him to design an online social network inspired by Google Circles. It went nowhere.

Still, Spiegel was getting noticed. Intuit's Scott Cook was impressed by an answer he gave while guest lecturing at Peter Wendell's popular graduate-level class, "Entrepreneurship and Venture Capital." "After class concluded, I commented on the intelligence and reasoning in this particular student's response," said Cook. "And Professor Wendell said, 'Well, you will be surprised to know he isn't an MBA student. He is an undergraduate who is auditing this class.'" Cook quickly hired Spiegel to work on an Intuit project that broadcasts Web-based information via SMS texts in India.

Spiegel, however, was in too much of a rush to remain content as an apprentice. In the summer of 2010, he and Murphy developed Future Freshman, a suite of online software to help parents, high schoolers, and guidance counselors manage college admissions. "It ended up being this unbelievably full-featured website," Murphy recalled. One problem: "We got, like, maybe five people on the service," said Spiegel.

That's when fate, in the form of another fraternity brother, Reggie Brown, stepped into Spiegel's room to discuss a photo he wished he hadn't sent someone. The ensuing set of events makes *The Social Network* look like C-SPAN2.

WHILE OWNERSHIP OF SNAPCHAT remains hotly disputed, all sides seem to agree on the genesis: Brown said something to the effect of "I wish there was an app to send disappearing photos." Brown refused to speak to *Forbes*, citing pending litigation, but his side of the story comes through via numerous court documents, including a leaked deposition. According to Brown, Spiegel became "physically animated" and repeatedly called Brown's remark "a million-dollar idea." (Spiegel acknowledged he was excited, but won't comment about the "million-dollar idea" line.) That night they set out to find a developer. Brown claimed two candidates declined; regardless, they settled on Murphy, who had just graduated.

The original roles were fairly defined: Murphy as CTO, Brown as CMO, Spiegel as CEO, honing the idea as part of a design class he was taking. The first iteration was a clunky website that required users to upload a photo and set a timer before sending. The eureka moment only came when the idea migrated to mobile. "At some point it was like, 'Hey, there's a camera on your phone,'" Spiegel said. "'Wouldn't that be easier?'"

The class culminated in a presentation to a panel of venture capitalists. Brown came up with a name for the app, Picaboo, and Murphy put in eighteen-hour days to get a working prototype. "The feedback was basically, 'Hmmmm. Well, thank you for showing us your project,'" recalled Spiegel. One investor suggested he partner with Best Buy. Many wondered why anyone would want to send a disappearing photo.

The first version debuted in the iOS App Store on July 13, 2011 . . . to yawns. "The Instagram fairy tale"—the app had 25,000 downloads on the first day—"that was not us, unfortunately," Murphy said. The team had worked around a potentially fatal flaw—the fact that recipients can take a screenshot, rendering a disappearing image permanent—by building in a notification if your picture has been captured, a potent social deterrent. Still, by the end of the summer Picaboo had only 127 users. Pathetic. Brown toyed with positioning the app as a sexting tool. ("Picaboo lets you and your boyfriend send photos for peeks and not keeps!" reads a draft of a press release he wrote.) Murphy's parents implored him to get a real job. And Spiegel apparently began pushing to shake up the team. According to Brown's deposition, he overheard Spiegel and Murphy plotting to replace him.

The breaking point came when equity was being finalized. A month later, Brown, back home in South Carolina, called his two partners and laid out his case. He wanted around 30 percent, according to Murphy's deposition, and listed his contributions: the initial idea, the Picaboo name, and the now-famous ghost logo. Spiegel and Murphy countered that he didn't deserve anywhere close to that. When Brown claimed that he had "directed [the] talents" of Spiegel and Murphy, Murphy remembered, an enraged Spiegel hung up. Spiegel and Murphy changed administrative passwords for the app and cut off contact except for a few tense e-mails about a pending patent. Brown was out, relegated to something of a Snapchat version of the Winklevoss twins or Eduardo Saverin. (Ironically, in their battle with Brown, Snapchat hired the legal team that pursued the Winklevoss claim against Facebook.)

Now a two-man operation, Picaboo changed its name to Snapchat after receiving a cease-and-desist letter from a photo-book company with the same name. "That was like the biggest blessing ever," said Spiegel. But even as he and Murphy added photo caption capabilities, they seemed destined to replicate their Future Freshman experience: a technically competent product that virtually no one wanted. Spiegel returned to Stanford for his senior year; Murphy took a coding job at Revel Systems, an iPad point-of-sale company in San Francisco.

But that fall Snapchat began to exhibit a pulse. As user numbers approached 1,000, an odd pattern emerged: App usage peaked between 9:00 a.m. and 3:00 p.m.—school hours. Spiegel's mother had told her niece about the app, and the niece's Orange County high school had quickly embraced Snapchat on their school-distributed iPads, since Facebook was banned. It gave them all the ability to pass visual notes during class—except, even better, the evidence vanished. Usage doubled over the holidays as those students received new, faster iPhones, and users surged that December, to 2,241. By January, users numbered 20,000; by April, 100,000.

But with growth came server bills. While Spiegel helped cover some of them with money from his grandfather, Murphy had to fork over half his paycheck. As monthly expenses approached $5,000, the guys needed a bailout.

Lightspeed Venture Partners' Jeremy Liew came to the rescue.

His partner's daughter relayed how Snapchat had become as popular as Instagram and Angry Birds at her Silicon Valley high school. But Spiegel and Murphy proved difficult to track down; their website had no contact information, and no one was listed on the company's LinkedIn page. Liew finally did a "Whois" lookup to find the owner of the Web domain, linked the obscure LLC that it was registered under to Spiegel and eventually tracked him down via Facebook. "His profile picture was with Obama," shrugged Spiegel. "So I thought he seemed legit."

In April 2012, Lightspeed put in $485,000 at a valuation of $4.25 million. "That was the greatest feeling of all time," said Spiegel. "There is nothing that will replace that." On the day the money went through, he sat in a machine-shop class busily refreshing the Wells Fargo app on his iPhone. In a final homage to Zuckerberg, when the money appeared he walked up to the professor and dropped out of the class and Stanford, a few weeks from graduation.

SNAPCHAT HAS MOVED THREE times since the initial investment, as the company grew, by early 2014, to a still-lean seventy employees. The latest offices, in a former art studio a block from the Venice board-walk, are appropriately anonymous, with just a small ghost logo to identify it. Most of the development that has made it a viral sensation, however, took place in 2012, when the company was headquartered at Spiegel's dad's house. "He convinced us to drop out of Stanford and move down to L.A. over the course of a single conversation," said Daniel Smith, who was hired along with Kravitz.

The team worked around the clock, sleeping where they worked. (Smith lived in Spiegel's sister's room, with enough girlish orange and pink polka dots, Spiegel remembers, "to give you an anxiety attack.") "Bobby had a habit of pushing code changes and then going to sleep," said Spiegel, who then found himself on debugging duty. "I'd wake up in the morning and go, 'Oh my God!'" Added Murphy: "I still have nightmares about him stomping down the stairs."

The arrangement proved oddly effective. Said Lightspeed's Liew: "They can call bullshit on each other, which makes their ideas better." What emerged was an app that, rather than a tool for the likes of Facebook, can potentially challenge it. By both luck and design, Snapchat addresses three red flags for Facebook. First, it's more intimate and exclusive. Just as Facebook took the anonymous Internet and boiled it down to real people you knew, Snapchat narrows your world from Facebook "friends," which range from long-forgotten schoolmates to nagging aunts, to your network of phone contacts. People, in other words, you actually talk to.

Second, it's perceived as young and cool. Most teens can probably find a grandparent on Facebook. Snapchat's mobile-first roots give it credibility with the app generation, who increasingly view PCs the way their parents viewed black-and-white televisions.

And in the age of Snowden, parental Facebook monitoring, and "revenge porn" (exes who publicly post nude pictures of former lovers), the self-destruction feature has become increasingly resonant. "This isn't a silly little messaging app," insisted Liew. "It allows people to revert back to a time when they never had to worry about self-censorship."

An entire subindustry—so-called ephemeral, or temporary, social media—has emerged behind it. Besides Poke (which has largely faded), there's Clipchat (a Snapchat/Twitter hybrid), Wickr (disappearing texts), and dozens of other apps pushing the boundaries of digital communication back toward what a telephone call used to be—a way to communicate with little risk it will come back to bite you.

All of them, however, are stuck chasing Spiegel and Murphy, who have evolved Snapchat into something fun and easy. (Though, in 2014, Snapchat agreed with federal regulators to stop overpromising, given several workarounds, that messages will surely disappear forever.) To view a snap, users hold a finger on their phone screens, a feature designed to make it still more difficult for people to photograph the image with another camera. Disappearing video is now an option. And while teens have embraced a medium unreachable by prying parents or future employers, grownups are catching on. All told, Snapchat users in early 2014 were sending 400 million photos and videos each day, matching the daily uploads to Facebook and Instagram combined.

"We certainly didn't invest in this to flip it," said Mitch Lasky, a Snapchat board member and partner at venture capital firm Benchmark Capital, which led Snapchat's $13.5 million fundraising round in 2013 (they also raised $60 million from Institutional Venture Partners)—and invested in Twitter way back in 2009.

AMID THE ASTOUNDING GROWTH, valuations, and talk of an independent future, one key ingredient is missing: revenue. Asia offers a possible blueprint. There, a handful of wildly popular mobile messaging services upsell users with in-app purchases. Spiegel's party line, when discussing revenue, feels as if it's read from a script: "In-app transactions followed by advertising, that's the plan we're sticking to."

Drilling down through some of the companies that Spiegel cites raises more questions than answers. China's WeChat, a massive messaging app owned by the Chinese Internet behemoth Tencent, encourages users to subscribe to celebrity greetings and to purchase physical goods. But it's mostly a texting app, and the messages don't disappear. Korea's KakaoTalk and Japan's Line make most of their money via mobile games, which don't seem a natural fit with Snapchat. And, of course, digital goods, like premium sticker packages, emoticons, and animations, are also moneymakers in Asia, though Spiegel seems to disapprove. "It'll make sense in a Snapchat way," he said. "But it will not be stickers."

Advertising is similarly tricky. Snapchat's core strengths in gaining users (your privacy is protected and your images disappear!) cripple the targeted advertising that most social media companies rely on (Snapchat knows little more than e-mail, age, phone number—plus your ads disappear!).

But it has one advantage that virtually no other digital advertiser can claim: guaranteed engagement. Users must keep their fingers on a photo or video to view it—and that applies to any ads thrown their way. Snapchat can tell advertisers with absolute certainty whether their ads were viewed, a rare data point in the metric-driven world of digital advertising.

Like Facebook, the company can also charge businesses for setting up branded accounts. Acura, Taco Bell, and the New Orleans Saints have already used the app to debut new products and show behind-the-scenes footage. The company's Stories feature, which lets users display a compilation of snaps taken over the last twenty-four hours, is useful for brands looking to tell a longer story. Example: Online retailer Karmaloop used the feature to show clips of posing models sprinkled with discount codes and new items. Others, like frozen yogurt chain 16 Handles, have experimented with "exploding coupons."

Spiegel and Murphy, slow in their college days to adapt to emerging platforms, also seem keen to not make that mistake again. In September 2013, for example, Snapchat debuted on the Samsung Galaxy Gear smartwatch. "People haven't thought about use cases on new computing platforms," said Thomas Laffont, managing director of Coatue, the hedge fund that provided the latest $50 million infusion. "In one tap you take a photo, one more and you can share it. Imagine [the difficulty] trying to post on Instagram from a Google Glass device."

Ah, Instagram. Zuckerberg's Poke might be languishing, but he still has the last billion-dollar app to come out of Stanford. Kevin Systrom's $1 billion sale in 2013, in fact, is often held up as the reason Snapchat was right to turn down Facebook's preemptive billions. (Instagram would likely be worth as much as ten times more now.) Zuck is going after Snapchat again with a tweak to Instagram— Instagram Direct, a Snapchat knock-off with a key difference: The images don't vanish unless users go in and delete them.

Spiegel and Murphy have another headache: Brown's lawsuit, which asks for one-third of the company plus punitive damages. "It's definitely over a billion dollars we're seeking," said Luan Tran, one of Brown's three lawyers. Insiders say Snapchat is eager to try the case, but videos of depositions, presumably leaked by Brown's team, show Spiegel and Murphy far more equivocal and forgetful than their opponent. "I'm just hoping it gets resolved so it doesn't prove to be a distraction," said Benchmark's Lasky.

The proverbial "adults" have been brought in, including Philippe Browning, the vice president of monetization, nabbed from CBS, and COO Emily White, poached from the business division of, yes,

Instagram. But, tellingly, the company prevented *Forbes* from interviewing either of them.

So for now the doubters carry the day. "There's an almost ritual incantation when these things reach 50 million daily active users and people say, 'Well they're not making any revenue,'" said Lasky. "It's unfair to expect these things to generate revenue while growing so quickly." To his point, the same was said about Twitter and Facebook. But it was also intoned by the dot-com oracles on the eve of catastrophe fifteen years ago. Will Snapchat wilt like MySpace, get out at a peak valuation the way Mark Cuban sold Broadcast.com, or prove to be the next great social media IPO? We should get our answer by 2016, just in time for Spiegel to turn the ripe old age of twenty-five.

CHAPTER 14

Palmer Luckey, Oculus VR: Virtual Reality, Tangible Fortune

When *Forbes* magazine highlighted Palmer Luckey, a twenty-one-year-old video game tinkerer, on our annual "30 Under 30" list in January 2014, many readers chuckled. Barely old enough to drink, Luckey had a company with no revenues, not even a commercial product—just a prototype with a bizarre name, Oculus Rift. Less than three months later, however, no one was laughing. Mark Zuckerberg ponied up $2 billion in cash and stock to bring Oculus—or more specifically, Luckey's virtual reality headset—into the Facebook fold. But what makes Luckey's score so revolutionary isn't his precocious age or even the potential that "the Rift" holds to change how we view the world. Instead, as **David M. Ewalt** deftly shows, it's how he was able to create incredible value by enhancing the work of others, without paying them for it, and then crowdfund it through the wallets of others, without giving up any equity. The age of open-source entrepreneurship is upon us.

———

It's dark and creepy in the cargo hold of the *Sevastopol*; something could be hiding in here, and I'd never know it. As I walk between the piles of crates, I stop and peek around every corner. A noise makes my heart skip a beat. I tell myself it was just dripping water.

I shouldn't have been scared, since I knew this is just a video game—a demo of *Alien: Isolation*, an upcoming horror-adventure based on the decades-old movie. But I was also wearing a virtual reality headset called the Oculus Rift, and the Rift makes it real: The game filled my entire field of vision—when I turned my head to look around, the world moved with me. It felt like I was actually on a space station being stalked by one of those same creatures that stalked Sigourney Weaver. And that wasn't a good feeling.

There was another sound, and I turned to see a heavy blast door slide open at the end of a corridor. Behind it, there was a crouching, bipedal form, the size of a large man, covered in a shiny black exoskeleton. I stared, frozen, as the alien rose, closed the gap between us, and wrapped its arms around my body. Its dripping mouth opened, and inner jaws plunged toward my face.

An involuntary squeal of panic emitted from my mouth. From behind me—this time in the real world—I heard a laugh. Palmer Luckey, the twenty-one-year-old creator of the Oculus Rift, had been watching as I played. "You got eaten?" he chortled. "You didn't last very long."

Luckey had been preparing for a game like this since he was a kid—which wasn't that long ago. He started making virtual reality headsets when he was sixteen. At nineteen, he founded his company, Oculus VR. And now, finally old enough to drink, he sold this company for $2 billion to Facebook, despite the fact that his start-up had no revenue at the time, or even a commercial product. Instead, Zuckerberg ponied up that number, one as fantastical as the alien that had devoured me, for a simple reason: He believed that Luckey was on the verge of doing what generations of technologists before him tried and failed—bring virtual reality to the masses.

THE PATH TO THIS new world began in the setting of so many modern success stories, which has almost become a cliché: a California garage. But Palmer Luckey wasn't a striving Stanford graduate or dot-com refugee; he was an obsessed teenager, eldest of four children, the homeschooled son of a Long Beach car salesman and a stay-at-home mom, and he spent every spare minute with either video games (*Chrono Trigger* and *GoldenEye 64* were among his favorites) or science fiction (particularly high-tech fantasies like *The Matrix* and *The Lawnmower Man*.) These passions both led him to the same place. "Virtual reality is in so much science fiction, across a wide variety of stories, that even if you're not particularly interested in VR, if you're a sci-fi enthusiast you end up learning a lot about it," said Luckey. "That's what happened. I grew up my whole life thinking virtual reality was very cool, and I thought that it must exist in secret military labs somewhere."

The idea for immersive computer displays emerged in the 1960s. Early VR prototypes were primitive, bulky, and hugely expensive, built mainly for government and military applications like air force flight simulators. In the 1980s, the personal computer boom raised hopes for smaller, more consumer friendly headsets, and inspired new art that romanticized virtual worlds: Consumer interest in the technology took off after William Gibson's 1984 novel *Neuromancer*, and peaked when nearly a dozen related films (including *Johnny Mnemonic*, *Virtuosity*, and *Strange Days*) were released in 1995.

But while the movies sold tickets, the products went nowhere. Sometimes, excessive costs killed them in their infancy: In the early 1990s, Hasbro spent $59 million and more than three years developing a console and headset called the Home Virtual Reality System, before abandoning the project. CFO John O'Neill told the Associated Press that the gadget's $300 price tag would have priced it out of the consumer market.

More often, VR was doomed by technical problems. In 1996, Nintendo released a $180 video game console called the Virtual Boy, but its promise of three-dimensional graphics fell flat. The headset's red monochrome display, low resolution, and use of high-speed vibrating mirrors gave its users neck pains, dizziness, nausea, and headaches. Nintendo sold less than 800,000 units and discontinued the product after a year.

The teenage Luckey went hunting for evidence of this arcane technology. He scoured eBay sales for outdated and abandoned bits of VR hardware, and slowly amassed an impressive collection; in one score, he bought a $97,000 headset for only $87. To fund his efforts, he taught himself basic electronics, and made $30,000 by buying broken iPhones, repairing them, and flipping them for a profit.

From these failures, Luckey hacked something new. "I was modifying existing gear really heavily, using new lenses, trying to swap lenses from one system into another," said Luckey. "I built some shitty stuff."

With time, his work improved. In 2009—when he was only seventeen—Luckey started building the PR1, or Prototype One. "The entire optical system was all custom for that head-mounted display," he said. Meanwhile, college beckoned, and the home-schooler stayed close to home—Cal State, Long Beach, studying journalism, of all things. ("I wanted to be a tech journalist who understood how the technology worked.")

He kept working on VR systems in his free time, and in the summer of 2011 landed a part-time job working with virtual reality pioneer Mark Bolas at his lab in the Institute for Creative Technologies at the University of Southern California. "Without Mark, there would be no Oculus," said Jaron Lanier, a computer scientist who popularized the term "virtual reality." Bolas and his students had spent years refining hardware and software for VR headsets, and all their innovations were open-source; Luckey absorbed their wisdom and their technology, and quickly applied them to his own work.

In April 2012, nineteen-year-old Palmer Luckey completed the sixth prototype of his home-brewed VR rig. He named it after the gap he hoped it would bridge between the real world and the virtual: the Rift.

PALMER LUCKEY'S PRODIGIOUS SUCCESS could not have happened even a generation before. The open-source head start allowed him to begin his quest on second or even third base, for free, without legally owing anyone a penny. He then harnessed the hive to hone his thinking, collaborating in discussion groups like the forums of a website called MTBS3D, or "Meant to Be Seen in 3D." Each of his six prototypes was constructed with help from these online enthusiasts, and in turn, Luckey frequently helped solve technical problems for other members of the crew.

At least one of those forum members was no ordinary hobbyist. John Carmack made his first splash in the video game business when he cofounded id Software in 1991; over the following decade, he cemented a legendary reputation working as lead programmer on games including *Quake* and *Doom*. In April 2012, he posted for help modifying a Sony head-mounted display. Remembered Luckey: "We had a public discussion about why it would be very difficult to do . . . and then a couple weeks later, he contacted me in a private message and asked if he could buy or borrow one of my prototypes."

Luckey shipped out one of his Rifts. Two months later, at the annual E3 video game industry expo in Los Angeles, Carmack demoed a version of *Doom 3* on the hardware, and sung the rig's praises to anyone who would listen. Word of Luckey's gadget spread quickly. Brendan Iribe, then chief product officer at game-streaming company Gaikai, met him for a demo, and was so impressed he offered an investment on the spot. In July 2012, with a few hundred thousand dollars of Iribe's money as seed capital, Oculus VR was born.

The crowdsourcing, however, was just beginning. On August 1, 2012, Luckey launched a campaign to raise funds so he could build a new prototype and put it in the hands of software developers. He chose Kickstarter, a site that helps people fund passion projects— documentaries, invention prototypes, or whatnot. Donors at the time were banned from getting equity stakes, due to securities laws (the JOBS Act loosened up crowdfunding rules in 2013)—instead, they usually got anything from a T-shirt to the product they were helping to develop.

"If I'm an investor, what are the odds that I'm going to want to invest in this product, no matter how cool it seems, when there's such a precedent for virtual reality failing horribly?" Luckey said. "I think it would have been very hard to get any other investments . . . but with Kickstarter, you don't have people who are looking to make a large financial return; you have people who just want the thing you're making."

Under the terms of the fund-raiser, anyone who was paid at least $300 could receive their own Rift prototype, which they could use to start making software for the platform. Luckey knew there would be strong demand from VR enthusiasts, but was worried that community wasn't very big, so he set the campaign's goal at a relatively modest $250,000.

Once the public saw the Rift in action—and heard testimonials from video game luminaries like John Carmack, Valve cofounder Gabe Newell, and Epic Games design director Cliff Bleszinski— Luckey's fears melted away. The Kickstarter leapt past the $250,000 mark in less than two hours.

During the first day of the fund-raiser, Luckey was in Dallas, Texas, at the annual QuakeCon gaming convention, running demos of the Rift for interested players. "We were probably the smallest booth at the whole show," said Luckey. "We didn't have any signage, just a black table. And we had a line that was over two hours long the entire weekend. That's when I realized, 'Oh man, this is gonna be huge. Ordinary people are interested in virtual reality, not just us crazy sci-fi nerds.'"

As the Kickstarter boomed—after thirty days, it topped out at

$2.4 million, from 9,522 backers—it became clear that Oculus VR was going to have legs as a company. And Luckey, unlike other wunderkinds, saw his limitations as an executive. His seed investor, Brendan Iribe, became CEO. Shortly after, John Carmack left a post at ZeniMax Media to become CTO. Luckey's title would simply be "founder," and he would continue in a grander, more general role, as the face of virtual reality.

THE KICKSTARTER HOME RUN provided more than just a war chest (and one that didn't carry any dilution, other than being on the hook for hundreds of prototypes). It turned Luckey, and Oculus, into video game world superstars. At events like South by Southwest and the Game Developers Conference, attendees continued to stand in line for hours to get demos of the Rift.

Venture capitalists started lining up, too. In June 2013, Oculus closed a $16 million Series A funding round co-led by Spark Capital and Matrix Partners, with participation from Founders Fund and Formation 8. The pre-money valuation was $30 million. Six months later, Andreessen Horowitz led a $75 million Series B, with additional capital from all four original firms at a valuation likely in the $300 million range.

"The dream of VR had been around so long that most people in the technology community had given up on it," says Chris Dixon, a partner at Andreessen Horowitz. "When we first met Palmer, we saw he not only continued to believe in the dream but also understood how to put all the key underlying technologies together to make it a reality."

Valuing a twenty-one-year-old's prototype headset at $300

million struck many as euphoric. Within weeks, though, it was proven to be a genius investment. Facebook's Mark Zuckerberg had reached out to Luckey in his preferred fashion, via e-mail, a few months earlier. The older wunderkind and the younger bonded over technology and, yes, sci-fi, and eventually, Zuck came to the Oculus office to try the Rift.

"We started off talking to Zuckerberg because we wanted to show off our stuff," said Luckey. "He's a big fan of virtual reality, and I think he believes in the same vision that we have, that everyone in the world is going to be exposed to VR." Zuck in turn told Luckey and Iribe that they may have stumbled into the next generation of computing—an entirely new way for people to communicate, rather than just a new route to Facebook.

A month after that visit, the two teams spent a week hammering out a deal, which eventually totaled $2 billion, including $400 million in cash up front, Facebook stock to fill out the rest, and another $300 million in incentives. Luckey was enamored by the credibility Facebook could bring. "I have been a skeptic of Oculus," said Michael Pachter, an analyst at Wedbush Securities, tellingly. "And then Facebook came along. Facebook is looking at the hardware as a platform to do other things than gaming—maybe instruction, teaching—and Facebook will get third parties to make content. Now Oculus can realize a broader strategy, with a big bank account behind them."

Indeed, that war chest was an equal consideration. "Let's say you want to sell a million of these things," said Luckey. "That means you have to have a few hundred million in cash just sitting around to build them." Facebook, in other words, could actually make VR a mainstream consumer technology.

Facebook could also make Luckey rich. *Forbes* estimates that Luckey owned around 25 percent of Oculus VR, meaning the twenty-one-year-old was suddenly worth a half billion dollars.

SO WHAT STANDS IN the way of making virtual reality a reality? First, a lawsuit: ZeniMax charged in May 2014 that its former employee, John Carmack, gave Oculus proprietary information (Oculus denies the charges).

Second, there's competition. In March 2014, Sony announced it was developing its own VR headset, codenamed Project Morpheus, for its PlayStation 4 video game console. "We see it first and foremost as another way of building vibrancy and value into the PlayStation ecosystem," said Andrew House, president and CEO of Sony Computer Entertainment. "VR is very hot, and not just for games. Non-game people are just coming out of the woodwork because they're interested in this."

Google and Amazon, meanwhile, wait in the wings. Google so far has shown more interest in augmented reality—inserting computer displays into the real world, à la Google Glass—than wholly virtual worlds. Amazon has been silent on the topic, but virtual shopping malls are one of the most obvious and promising applications of VR—instead of looking at a two-dimensional photograph of a product, you could pop on a headset and handle it, play with it, or try it on.

The final bit of caution: In 1985, computer scientist Jaron Lanier left his job at Atari to found VPL Research, the first company to ever sell a VR headset. It filed for bankruptcy two years before Palmer Luckey was born. "Recent events are weird for me in a way that the folks at Oculus couldn't possibly know, in that so many of the designs, the headlines, the little intrigues, and the chatter are similar to what I experienced over thirty years ago," said Lanier. "All I can say is that I wish Mr. Luckey all the success in the world."

Luckey is aware of this failure, and many others. This time, however, he thinks the technology is finally ready. "I don't think there are any comparable products right now," said Luckey. "We've got the best team in the virtual reality industry, we've got a lot of the best people in the games industry, we've got big partnerships with hardware manufacturers and game developers. I think we're on the path of making the world's best virtual reality hardware . . . and I think the consumer product is going to be way ahead of anything anyone else can do for the next couple of years."

And even if it's not, Luckey is determined to pursue his dream. Oculus has been in acquisition mode in 2014, buying Carbon Design Group, a Seattle-based product design studio, and RakNet, a game networking engine that, fittingly, is open-source. Cash is no longer an issue for Luckey. And he certainly has the time horizon. "Five years from now, I don't know if everyone's going to have a headset," he said. "But I'll be doing this until it happens, or until I die."

CHAPTER 15

Adi Tatarko, Houzz: Breaking into the Boy's Club

Silicon Valley has a woman problem. The number of tech start-ups helmed by women is pathetic when measured against the potential talent. And the "bro" culture, an unfortunate by-product of a place and time where young men reign supreme, can be even worse. That's what makes Adi Tatarko especially interesting. Yes, she and her husband have, with far less fanfare than their peers, quickly built up a personal fortune approaching $1 billion, thanks to their ascendant home design site, Houzz. But **George Anders** details how Tatarko faces hurdles and dilemmas that her male peers simply don't.

Silicon Valley start-ups tend to get cranking in the rough-and-tumble domains of male engineers: garages, college fraternity rooms, or high-powered tech incubators. Adi Tatarko started Houzz, a Web-based home-design community valued in 2014 at more than $2 billion, in a beanbag chair in her children's bedroom.

She and her husband, software engineer Alon Cohen, had wanted to upgrade their kitchen and add an extra room to their sunny three-bedroom ranch house in Palo Alto. Yet after two and a half years of flipping through magazines and meeting with architects, they remained stumped, and were especially frustrated by the lack of an online one-stop shop of design ideas. So the couple decided to build one. He worked in a nook next to the kitchen, coding the site. She drummed up content, coaxing a former *Sunset* magazine editor, Sheila Schmitz, to join her. In one of their earliest chats, back in 2009, Schmitz recalls, Tatarko scrunched down on that beanbag chair and spelled out the guiding philosophy for a site that would ignore everyone else's proven formulas for e-commerce and opinionated blogging, in favor of a maverick approach that encouraged innocent window-shopping. Five years later, Houzz was one of the two hundred most visited websites in the United States, ahead of the likes of *People* magazine, United Airlines, and CNBC.

From the family setting to soft-sell strategy, it was an unusual start. But Houzz is an unusual company. Of the 150 largest companies in Silicon Valley in 2013, according to a study by the law firm Fenwick and West, more than 43 percent didn't even have one woman on the board of directors (versus just 2 percent of the S&P 100), and over 45 percent had nary a single female executive (S&P 100: just 16 percent). Company founders? A rough survey indicates that just one in twenty venture-backed start-ups is woman-run, and those that get off the ground raise perhaps two-thirds as much money. Some of that bias stems from an education system that dissuades girls from science and math; some of it comes from Silicon

Valley's geek-cool "bro" culture. Yet all of it seems to work as an advantage for Tatarko, a verbal tornado who is less likely be talked over than even the most garrulous, deep-voiced man. For the Houzz CEO, her gender helps her understand her market, and create a culture that's at once rambunctious ("She has no boundaries," whispers one of her male investors) and inclusive (she serves cake for each of her two hundred employees' birthdays).

"I'm a woman, so I'm more emotional," said the forty-one-year-old CEO. "I need things here and now." Her employees sometimes do impersonations of Tatarko, declaring some big new business goal, while her forty-three-year-old husband, the president and chief technologist, frets that she has promised too much. These skits (and reality) always end the same way. The deadline arrives; Houzz's performance surpasses even Tatarko's ambitious forecast, and the CEO rises to her feet to gleefully declare: "We did it, even though Alon said we couldn't!"

IT'S NOT A COINCIDENCE that one of America's most successful women tech entrepreneurs hails from Israel, a country correctly dubbed "Start-up Nation," its tech dynamism fueled in part by the training and maturity forged from mandatory military service—for men *and* women. Growing up in Israel in the 1980s, Tatarko drew inspiration from a mother who was a real-estate broker and a grandmother who had been a prominent fashion designer for decades, who flew to Paris on her own for exhibitions when women simply didn't do such things. "I remember coming to my grandmother's home and being fascinated that she was juggling everything so well," Tatarko recalled. "She had great support from the rest of the family, and I was so proud of her."

An international studies major at Jerusalem's Hebrew University, Tatarko graduated in 1996 with hazy plans to travel abroad and "make ugly places beautiful." Rambling through Thailand with two girlfriends, she ended up on a fifteen-hour bus ride from Bangkok to the island of Koh Samui. ("We didn't have enough money to buy plane tickets," she recalls.) She sat in the front, keeping her distance from three young Israeli men in the back of the bus. But the driver wanted the front seats empty, so he tugged her toward the back and deposited her next to a tall redhead, Alon Cohen.

"We talked nonstop for the whole bus ride," Tatarko recalled. "It was like four dates, one after another. It was wonderful." They stuck together for the rest of the vacation. When they got back to Israel, they opened a small tech-services company together, PROmis Software. In 1998, they married, and shortly afterward, they moved to New York, where both saw better career opportunities. The kept heading west: By 2001, they were in Silicon Valley, where Cohen had landed an engineering job at eBay.

Cohen wound up heading up engineering teams that worked on everything from monetization strategies to application programming interfaces, or APIs, which make it easier for outsiders to work with eBay's data—skills that would eventually accelerate Houzz. Tatarko's ambitions took a backseat: Her first son was born in 2002, and two more followed. She worked part-time as an investment adviser for Commonwealth Financial, coaching clients on how to manage their money.

Then Houzz started to take shape, proving the core truth of this latest gold rush: Even after a twenty-year stampede to create consumer Internet start-ups, plenty of big, unexplored opportunities still exist. The richest cluster of this latest digital boom involves community sites like Pinterest and Twitter, which nimbly connect the curious with the sharers. Such start-ups are hopelessly unsuited to bringing in revenue at first. But if they can grow to attract millions of users, all the usual opportunities to sell ads, data, and goods spring to life. With $150 billion spent each year on home improvement just in the United States, Houzz was an especially fruitful example of how this dynamic plays out.

The new company began imperceptibly in 2006, when Cohen bought the rights to www.houzz.com for twenty dollars. "We wanted a five-letter domain name that had something to do with home improvement," he explained. The natural choice, www.house.com, was long gone. But he and Tatarko decided that their concoction would suffice; it combined the terms "house" and "buzz" in a way that they hoped would seem clever. They hardly used the domain name until 2008. That's when Tatarko started collecting designer photos and asking other parents at her boys' schools if they might want to look at home-improvement photos, too.

Think of Houzz as the triumph of the innocents. The site lacks the trend-spotting insistence of an architecture magazine; it's missing the "buy now" exhortations of a big-league e-commerce site. But those omissions mean Houzz sidesteps the egos and pushiness that usually plague interior design. Houzz is an explorer's haven, letting jittery homeowners browse for as long as they choose, gradually sharpening their tastes and budgets until they can say with confidence: "Here's what we want."

While the traffic originally came mostly from the Bay Area, the site quickly attracted a global following. More unexpectedly, architects and interior designers began serenading Tatarko and Cohen, out of the blue, clamoring to post photo albums, giving the site a seemingly unlimited supply of free content and ideas. "Houzz has become as much of a tool in how architects communicate with clients as a pencil or a T-square," said Richard Buchanan, a high-end architect near Philadelphia, who took early note when his clients began showing up at his office with tidy digital "IdeaBooks" from Houzz.

In 2009, the couple faced a crossroads. Houzz couldn't be a weekend hobby anymore. The fast-growing company needed twenty servers to sustain its expected data load. It needed full-time engineers and full-time editors. Houzz also needed far more cash than the $2,000 a month Tatarko and Cohen were dribbling into it.

Where to turn? "Adi and I were scared of venture capitalists then," Cohen recalled. It was clear that the couple could turn a small profit in a hurry by jamming the site full of ads, or by setting up some pay-to-see features that would make it harder for architects and clients to get connected on their own. But neither of them wanted to do so. Tatarko was especially adamant. She wanted to spend at least a year or two making Houzz the friendliest, smoothest site possible, before worrying at all about what the business model should be. Neither of the founders wanted to take money from a financier who might arm-twist them to put profits ahead of quality.

Safety arrived in the form of Oren Zeev, a Silicon Valley angel investor who was recommended to Tatarko and Cohen by a mutual Israeli-born acquaintance. He promised the Houzz founders that they would stay in charge. He would only look for ways to make their vision come true. In November 2009, he led a syndicate of investors that took a 35 percent stake in Houzz for $2 million. Other investments began streaming in, including $1 million–plus from

David Sacks, the founder of office-productivity tool Yammer, who came across Houzz while gut-rehabbing a San Francisco town house. "We'd start scrolling through pictures, and we couldn't stop," he recalled.

Those investments proved quite astute. Houzz doesn't disclose its operating results, but people familiar with its books say the company has operated at a very modest burn rate since 2011, in spite of making only modest attempts to monetize its business. The site could take a cut of commerce or referral revenue; it also could step up what right now are fairly tiny efforts in preferred listings. Today, many thousands of architects and designers pay about $2,500 a year, each, for premium listings in Houzz's regional directories. "I don't think we could get that many business leads any other way," said Mike Close, who runs Spinnaker Development, a luxury homebuilder in Orange County, California. "In fact, we're now updating our Houzz profile even before we add something to our website." They could increase their push among major manufacturers and retailers, with the likes of Ikea and Kohler already on board.

Instead, they continue to focus on site quality. And investors clearly buy into the money that will follow: Tatarko and Cohen have raised nearly $200 million in venture capital, culminating in a $150 million round that was negotiated in the first half of 2014. "We like founders who build companies to solve problems in their own lives, even if they aren't experts in the field," says Alfred Lin, a Sequoia Capital partner who led an initial venture investment in Houzz in 2011. "They unpack issues in a way that people in the industry have never unpacked them. They see things that everyone else misses."

Such vision can prove highly lucrative. This most recent round values Houzz at about $2.3 billion. Tatarko and Cohen's stake likely approaches $1 billion.

NOBODY ASKS MALE EXECUTIVES about work-life balance. But when Tatarko, while running one of the world's fast-growing start-ups, had a third son in 2013, it weighed on her. "I'm trying, I'm trying," Tatarko exclaimed at one point, in the midst of an interview mostly about Houzz, before remarking to no one in particular: "I hope I'm doing the right thing."

"There are things I can't do anymore. I used to cook every night. Now, someone else is using my recipes to cook for us." She's been reading Harry Potter novels to her second son as a bedtime treat for both of them, and that makes her smile. Still, she says, there are times she wakes up at 2:00 a.m., with the twin pressures of parenting and corporate leadership weighing on her. "I'll think: Did I schedule that playdate yet? And then I'll suddenly realize that there's another slide I need to make for the next board meeting."

And having a cofounder that doubles as your husband represents a dynamic intense even by Silicon Valley sleep-in-your-office standards. "This is hard," said their original financier, Oren Zeev. "They're juggling. Other than work and family, they really don't have a life." Other Silicon Valley CEOs take the work-hard, play-hard ethos seriously, weaving in conferences in Davos and Aspen with charitable boards and vacation homes. Not Tatarko or Cohen. They run a company, they connect with their kids, and they catch a few hours of sleep. That's it. Some nights Tatarko works late and Cohen dashes home to join the boys for dinner. Other evenings they reverse roles.

Even in the office, there's a sense that Tatarko and Cohen are constantly trying to fit thirty hours of activities into a twenty-four-hour day. Her sparse white desk sits in one corner of the company's giant, open-plan offices. Surrounded by editorial employees, she focuses on international expansion. Nearly 30 percent of the site's visitors already are from outside the United States, most of whom arrived by chance. In 2014, Houzz was in the process of opening offices in London and Sydney, and translating the site into German and French. Great design, Tatarko argues, can happen anywhere in the world, and good ideas are good ideas, no matter what time zone they come from.

Cohen, meanwhile, sits off in another corner, in the heart of engineering-land. Yes, it's a pretty site, but there's obsessive technology behind it. He and developer Guy Shaviv have filed a patent on some of Houzz's features, such as little green information tags that are attached to sinks, light fixtures, and the like, which offer viewers a chance to click for more details. To avoid having the tags look like aggressive advertisements, Shaviv arranged for them to sway back and forth in the mobile version, like tiny Christmas tree ornaments. Hidden algorithms allow for more than a hundred different pendulum arcs that can govern each tag, and no two wiggle at the same rate. Cohen's latest obsession: a new version of their iPad app, which already allows designers and architects to leave their binders at home.

Tatarko and Cohen remain in their own worlds each day until noon, when they break for an hour to get lunch together. This isn't a romantic escape—the conversation generally covers everything from site design to the latest about a sick child. Houzz engineer Ofir Zwebner, who has known Cohen and Tatarko for about a decade, said there's a "sweet bickering" between the two that helps them navigate through just about any challenge. They don't pretend that everything's going perfectly. Instead, they jostle through each new challenge, knowing that with a little give-and-take, they'll find the right answer once again. By 1:00 p.m., they're back to their separate corners of the office.

Boundaries matter in a family that's constantly feeling the tugs of conflicting demands. A while back, the couple's older boys complained that even when their parents showed up at home, their minds remained at work—and their fingers remained stuck on their smartphones. So, Tatarko says, there's a new rule at home now, calling for everyone to unplug from devices during family time. Parents put down their smartphones; the children let go of game consoles and iPads.

"Doing a start-up with kids is a lot more difficult," said Cohen. Two shifts of nannies provide backup child care throughout most waking hours. But there are many moments that the parents don't want to delegate at all. Cohen plays basketball regularly with his oldest son, Ben. To the parents' surprise, when they began talking about remodeling their driveway, Ben confronted them with a Houzz Idea-Book showing all the different ways that the driveway could be transformed into a partial basketball court. Parking their cars off-street might become impossible. But that wasn't his problem.

"What could we do?" Tatarko shrugged. "We arranged for him to have a meeting with the architect. And the architect listened very seriously to Ben's ideas. Everything needs to change all the time. They're growing, and the company is growing, too."

CHAPTER 16

Jan Koum, WhatsApp:
The Face of the American Dream

It's hard to come up with the proper superlative for what Jan Koum pulled off in founding WhatsApp and then selling it to Facebook for $19 billion. Silicon Valley's most successful startup ever? The greatest tech deal of the century? Both are likely true, but the one I think holds the most weight: the greatest rags-to-riches saga in American history.

While that's more debatable, Koum, now thirty-nine, inarguably belongs in the top ten, given the size and speed of the fortune and his background. He was born in Ukraine, outside Kiev, and emigrated here as a sullen teen. Brought up as an only child, he lived with his mother on welfare in Mountain View, before she succumbed to cancer. Alone, with not even a high school degree, Koum became, in the truest sense, a child of this country.

For someone who processes the conversations of more than half a billion people around the world, Koum remains a very private man. It took **Parmy Olson** eighteen months to convince him to speak with her for this story, and he hasn't talked to anyone publicly since. But for several months, Koum and Olson chatted and met regularly, and it so happened that the conversations overlapped with the evolution of the tech-deal-to-end-all-tech deals, resulting in a delicious tick-tock peek into business history. The story appeared within hours of the deal's completion, and someone in the company, for added effect, immediately "WhatsApp'd" Olson a photo. It was of Koum, signing on the dotted line—effectively giving himself a fortune, even after taxes, of $6.8 billion—against the door of the welfare office he frequented as a teen. The American Dream is alive and well in Silicon Valley.

"**G**et together?"

The subject line of the e-mail was like every other come-on that hit Jan Koum's in-box in the spring of 2012. He was pounded daily by investors who wanted a piece of his company, WhatsApp. Hatched on his birthday, February 24, in 2009, WhatsApp was emerging as a global phenomenon. Some 90 million people were using it to text and send photos for free. No social utility had ever grown as fast. Facebook had only 60 million users by its third birthday. And at the time, close to half of WhatsApp users were returning daily.

Koum looked at the e-mail sender: Mark Zuckerberg. Now, that was a first. The Facebook founder had been using WhatsApp and wanted him over for dinner. Koum stalled, then finally wrote back saying he was traveling soon and dealing with server issues. Zuckerberg suggested they meet before Koum left. Koum forwarded the reply to his cofounder, Brian Acton, and his sole venture backer, Jim Goetz, a partner at Sequoia Capital, adding the word: "Persistent!"

Take the meeting, Acton said: "When someone of Mark's status contacts you directly, you answer the phone."

Koum had lunch with Zuckerberg later that month at Esther's German Bakery, chosen for its discreet back patio and location, twenty miles away from Facebook's campus. Over their meal Zuckerberg said he admired what Koum had built and hinted at his interest in combining their two firms.

So began the most lucrative, two-year courtship in technology history, one in which admiration led to friendship and then, in a last-minute hurry, to an unprecedented transfer of wealth, all signed and sealed on the door of the welfare office Koum once haunted. In early 2014, Facebook bought WhatsApp for $4 billion in cash, $12 billion in stock (8.5 percent of the company) plus $3 billion in restricted shares. The deal cemented Zuckerberg as tech's new billionaire-maker. Koum, a shy but brilliant engineer who had moved from Ukraine to the U.S. with nary even a degree, joined the Facebook board and, after taxes, pocketed $6.8 billion. His cofounder, Brian Acton, a mild-mannered forty-three-year-old ex-Yahoo engineer who got turned down for jobs at Twitter and Facebook, came away with $3 billion after tax. The deal, he said, left him "astonished." Sequoia Capital, the only venture firm to taste a part of this deal, walked away with $3.5 billion—a sixty-fold return on its $58 million investment.

The numbers were crazy for a company with only fifty-six employees and roughly $20 million in revenue, but it made sense for Facebook. WhatsApp is one of the world's most commonly used utilities after e-mail and the telephone and is now rolling out voice calling. Its 480 million users have already erased $33 billion in SMS revenue from wireless carriers that got rich and fat charging per text. WhatsApp charges nothing for the first year and then asks you to pay $1 a year thereafter. No ads, no stickers, no premium upgrades. In later discussions Zuckerberg promised the WhatsApp founders "zero pressure" to make money, saying, "I would love for you guys to connect four to five billion people in the next five years."

WhatsApp could eventually make Zuck a lot of money. It costs WhatsApp five cents to support each user, and it's charging customers in only a handful of countries, like the U.S. and Britain, where mobile payments are relatively mature. WhatsApp believes $1 billion in annual revenue is within reach by 2017 as the service grows and billing falls into place. Insiders say the app could also start charging airlines or companies like Uber for the right to send messages into WhatsApp with user permission.

The big risk, as always, is a mass exodus of users to the next new thing. That doesn't seem likely right now. WhatsApp, Acton confirmed, was signing up a million new users per day in the early months of 2014. Everyone in Hong Kong with a smartphone uses WhatsApp. In the United Arab Emirates you can watch *WhatsApp Academy* on TV. In the Netherlands, where 9.5 million people (more than half the population) actively use it, "Whatsappen" is now a verb in the Dutch dictionary, meaning to send a WhatsApp message. Brazil's professional soccer players use its group-chat feature to organize labor strikes during games. "Sometime in the not-too-distant future," said Sequoia's Goetz, "WhatsApp is likely to eclipse all SMS traffic across the globe."

TO UNDERSTAND WHY WHATSAPP got where it is today, you only have to walk a couple of blocks from its unmarked headquarters in Mountain View to a disused white building across the railroad tracks, the former location of North County Social Services, where Koum once stood in line to collect food stamps.

Koum was born and raised in the small town of Fastiv, outside of Kiev, Ukraine, the only child of a housewife and a construction manager who built hospitals and schools. Electricity and hot water were limited. His parents rarely talked on the phone, in case it was tapped by the state. It sounds bad, but Koum still pines for the rural life he once lived, and it's one of the main reasons he's so vehemently against the hurly-burly of advertising.

At sixteen, in 1992, Koum and his mother immigrated to Mountain View to flee a troubling political and anti-Semitic environment, and got a small two-bedroom apartment through government assistance. His dad, who died in 1997, never made it over. Koum's mother had stuffed their suitcases with pens and a stack of twenty Soviet-issued notebooks to avoid paying for school supplies in the U.S. She took up babysitting, and Koum swept the floor of a grocery store to help make ends meet. When his mother was diagnosed with cancer, they lived off her disability allowance. Koum spoke English well enough but disliked the casual, flighty nature of American high school friendships; in Ukraine you went through ten years with the same, small group of friends. There, he says, "you really learn about a person."

Koum was kicked out of high school and had to attend an

alternative program, but by eighteen had taught himself computer networking by purchasing manuals from a used-book store and returning them when he was done. He joined a hacker group called w00w00 on the EFnet Internet relay chat network, squirreled into the servers of Silicon Graphics, and chatted with Napster cofounder Shawn Fanning.

He enrolled at San Jose State University and moonlighted at Ernst & Young as a security tester. In 1997, Koum found himself sitting across a desk from Acton, Yahoo employee number 44, to inspect the company's advertising system. "You could tell he was a bit different," recalled Acton. "He was very no-nonsense, like 'What are your policies here? What are you doing here?'" Other Ernst & Young people were using touchy-feely tactics like gifting bottles of wine. "Whatever," said Acton.

It turned out Koum liked Acton's no-nonsense style, too: "Neither of us has an ability to bullshit," said Koum. Six months later Koum interviewed at Yahoo and got a job as an infrastructure engineer. He was still at San Jose State University when, two weeks into his job at Yahoo, one of the company's servers broke. Yahoo cofounder David Filo called his cell phone for help. "I'm in class," Koum answered discreetly. "What the fuck are you doing in class?" Filo said. "Get your ass into the office." Filo had a small team of server engineers and needed all the help he could get. "I hated school anyway," Koum said. He dropped out.

When Koum's mother died of cancer in 2000, the young Ukrainian was suddenly alone. He credits Acton with reaching out and offering support. "He would invite me to his house," Koum remembered. The two went skiing and played soccer and Ultimate Frisbee.

Over the next nine years the pair watched Yahoo ride multiple ups and downs. Neither of them liked dealing with ads. "You don't make anyone's life better by making ads work better," said Acton. In his LinkedIn profile, Koum unenthusiastically describes his last three years at Yahoo with the words, "Did some work."

In October 2007 they left for a year of decompression, traveling around South America and playing more Frisbee. Ironically, both got rejected for jobs at Facebook. Koum was eating into his $400,000 in savings from Yahoo and drifting. Then, in January 2009, he bought an iPhone and started using the App Store. Here was a new industry in the making. He visited the home of Alex Fishman, a Russian friend who would invite the Russian community to his place in West San Jose for weekly pizza and movie nights. Up to forty people sometimes showed up. The two of them stood for hours talking about Koum's idea for an app over tea at Fishman's kitchen counter.

"Jan was showing me his address book," recalled Fishman. "His thinking was it would be really cool to have statuses next to individual names of the people." The statuses would show if you were on a call, your battery was low or you were at the gym. Koum could build the guts of the service, but he needed an iPhone developer. So Fishman introduced Koum to Igor Solomennikov, a developer in Russia whom he'd found on RentACoder.com.

Koum almost immediately chose the name WhatsApp because it sounded like "What's up?" A week later, on his birthday, he incorporated WhatsApp in California. The code hadn't even been written yet. Koum spent days writing the software to synch his app with any phone number in the world, poring over a Wikipedia entry that listed international dialing prefixes—he would spend many infuriating months updating it for the hundreds of regional nuances.

Early WhatsApp kept crashing or getting stuck, and when

Fishman installed it on his phone, only a handful of people in his address book had downloaded it. Over ribs at Tony Roma's in San Jose, Fishman went over the problems, and Koum took notes in one of the Soviet-era notebooks his mother had brought over, which he'd saved for important projects. Koum almost gave up and muttered to Acton about the need to look for another job. "You'd be an idiot to quit now," said Acton. "Give it a few more months."

Help came from Apple when it launched push notifications in June 2009, letting app developers ping users when they weren't using an app. Koum updated WhatsApp so that each time you changed your status—"Can't talk, I'm at the gym"—it would notify everyone in your network. Fishman's Russian friends started using it to ping each other with jokey custom statuses like "I woke up late" or just "I'm on my way."

"At some point it sort of became instant messaging," said Fishman. "We started using it as 'Hey how are you?' And then someone would reply." Koum watched the changing statuses on a Mac Mini at his town house in Santa Clara and realized he'd inadvertently created a messaging service. "Being able to reach somebody halfway across the world instantly, on a device that is always with you, was powerful," said Koum.

The only other free texting service at the time was BlackBerry's BBM, but that only worked among BlackBerrys. There was Google's G-Talk and Skype, but WhatsApp was unique in that the login was your own phone number, with no password to memorize. In September 2009, Koum released a new version with a messaging component and watched his active users suddenly swell to 250,000.

He needed help and went to see Acton, who was still unemployed and dabbling in another startup idea that wasn't going anywhere. In

October Acton got five ex-Yahoo friends to invest $250,000 in seed funding and as a result was granted cofounder status and a stake. He officially joined that November. They worked off cheap Ikea tables in a subleased space in Evernote's converted warehouse in downtown Mountain View. They wore blankets for warmth. There was no sign for the office. "Their directions were 'Find the Evernote building. Go round the back. Find an unmarked door. Knock,'" said Michael Donohue, one of WhatsApp's first BlackBerry engineers, recalling his first interview.

With Koum and Acton working for free for the first few years, their biggest early cost was sending verification texts to users. The founders occasionally switched the app from free to "paid" so they wouldn't grow faster than their subscriber income. In December they updated WhatsApp for the iPhone to send photos and were shocked to see user growth increasing even with the $1 price tag on. "You know, I think we can actually stay paid," Acton told Koum.

By early 2011 WhatsApp was squarely in the top twenty of most countries' App Stores. (The U.S. was slow to catch on, with its proclivity for unlimited texting plans.) Koum and Acton were batting away all requests from investors. Acton saw VC funding as a bailout. But Sequoia partner Jim Goetz spent eight months working his contacts to get either founder to engage. He'd met with a dozen other messaging companies, such as Pinger, Tango, and Beluga, but it was clear WhatsApp was the leader, and to Goetz's surprise the startup was already paying corporate income taxes: "The only time I've seen that in my venture career." He eventually got Koum and Acton to meet. They barraged him with questions and told him ads would be verboten. They eventually agreed to take $8 million from Sequoia in April 2011 at an $80 million valuation.

Two years later, in February 2013, when WhatsApp's user base had swelled to about 220 million active users and its staff to thirty, Acton and Koum agreed it was time to raise some more money. "For insurance," says Acton, who recalled that his mother, who ran her own freight-forwarding businesses, used to lose sleep over paying the bills. "You never want to be in a position where you can't make payroll." They decided to hold a second funding round, in secret. Sequoia would invest another $50 million to up its stake to 25 percent, valuing WhatsApp at $1.5 billion. At the time, Acton took a screenshot of WhatsApp's bank balance and sent it to Goetz. It read $8.257 million, still in excess of all the money they'd received years before.

BACK IN 2012, BEFORE that $50 million round and all the craziness that would soon follow, Koum had time to mull over his lunch with Zuckerberg. He and Acton had $8 million in the bank and wanted nothing more than their independence, so Facebook's overtures from then on never turned into bids on paper. Zuckerberg and Koum instead became friends, meeting once a month or so for dinner.

For the next year WhatsApp focused on its march past 300 million users. In June 2013, the founders happened to meet Sundar Pichai, who oversees Android and Chrome at Google. They talked about their love of clean and simple digital products. At some point around early 2014, Pichai decided it would be good for Koum and Acton to meet his CEO, Larry Page. They agreed to meet on Tuesday, February 11.

On the Friday before that meeting, a WhatsApp staffer ran into

Facebook's head of business development, Amin Zoufonoun, and told him that Koum was meeting with Page imminently. Zoufonoun raced back to Facebook and set the wheels in motion to accelerate an acquisition offer that had already been in the works for some time. Zuckerberg got Koum over to his house Monday night and finally floated the idea of an acquisition that would leave WhatsApp independent and, crucially, make Koum a board member of Facebook. "It was a partnership, where I would help him make decisions about the company," Koum recalled. "The combination of everything that was discussed is what made it very interesting for us."

The next day Koum and Acton drove to Google's Mountain View headquarters and met with Page and Pichai in one of the company's gleaming white conference rooms. They talked for an hour about the world of mobile and WhatsApp's goals. "It was a pleasant conversation," said Koum. Page, he added, is "a smart guy."

When asked if he got the impression Page was interested in buying WhatsApp, Koum paused. "No," he said. Maybe there was a hint? "Maybe I'm not good at reading him."

If Page had been interested in buying WhatsApp, as some reports later indicated, his meeting may have been too little, too late. Things had already been set in motion at Menlo Park, and at WhatsApp the founders and their advisors were calculating how much they could conceivably ask for in deal talks. One source close to the company said WhatsApp's founders were more interested in independence than money, but another said they also believed themselves to be worth at least $20 billion, a number calculated by looking at the market capitalization of Twitter, WhatsApp's global user base, and the company's future plans for monetization.

That Thursday, Koum and Acton went to Zuckerberg's house for dinner at 7:00 p.m., where Acton met Zuckerberg for the first time. "One day I want you to become bigger than us in number of users," Zuckerberg told them. "What you guys do is a much more common-use case." Zuckerberg said he wanted them to keep doing what they were doing, but with the might of Facebook's legal, financial, and engineering resources.

At 9:00 p.m., Acton went home to tend to his young family. Koum and Zuckerberg played high-stakes poker. One source said that Zuckerberg offered a range of $15 billion and higher, and that Koum said he was looking for something closer to $20 billion. Facebook's founder asked for some time.

The following day, Friday, February 14, Koum and Acton posed for a photo shoot with *Forbes* at their office. When the photographer left at 6:30 p.m., Koum got into his Porsche and stopped at Zuckerberg's house for another meeting. Koum denied reports that he interrupted the Zuckerbergs' Valentine's Day meal. "It wasn't like there was dinner and candlelight, and I barged in through the door." Until then he had tended to leave the Zuckerbergs' house when Mark's wife, Priscilla Chan, came home from work. Over snacks, Koum and Zuckerberg hammered out the final details of the partnership and WhatsApp's all-important independence under Facebook, but the two weren't yet in agreement.

Finally, on Saturday night, Koum and Zuckerberg went from talking in the kitchen to the living room couch, before Zuckerberg offered $19 billion as well as deal terms that Koum liked. It was "something we can probably do on our end," Koum replied.

Koum waited for Zuckerberg to leave the room and got on the

phone to Acton, who was at home. It was 9:00 p.m. "I just want to check if you've made a decision either way," Koum said, giving his friend the finalized details. "Do you want to move forward?"

"I like Mark," Acton replied. "We can work together. Let's make this deal." Koum walked out of the room and found Zuckerberg. "I just talked to Brian," Koum said. "He thinks we should work together and that you're a good guy and we should do it."

The two of them shook hands and then hugged. Zuckerberg remarked it was "fucking exciting," and whipped out a bottle of Johnnie Walker Blue Label, which he knew was Koum's favorite Scotch. They each called their business-development directors to come over and finalize the process. About an hour later, Koum drove home in his Porsche and went to bed.

Lawyers and bankers raced through the weekend to get deal papers to sign by Wednesday morning before everyone broke for the annual Mobile World Congress in Barcelona. Rather than signing them at WhatsApp's headquarters, they drove two blocks, at Jim Goetz's suggestion, to 101 Moffett Boulevard, the abandoned building where Koum once collected food stamps as a teenager. Koum signed them on the main door.

When they got back to the office, Koum sent a WhatsApp message to "WhatsApp All," the chat group for all employees, saying there would be an all-hands meeting in the conference room at 2:00 p.m.

"Look, here's what's happening," he said after everyone had piled into the room. "We're merging with Facebook." Koum and Acton told their shocked employees they would be okay and still operate on their own. At 2:30 p.m. the conference-room door opened again and in walked Mark Zuckerberg. He spoke briefly with WhatsApp's small staff and shook hands. After a conference call with investors, Koum got back to work. "We still have a company to run," he said matter-of-factly.

NOW IT'S DOWN TO Zuckerberg and Koum to figure out how to make WhatsApp worth the $19 billion Facebook paid for it. The first move was to make sure the app keeps working. The Saturday after the deal was announced, people around the world slammed WhatsApp's servers with new sign-ups. The app suffered a four-hour outage. The founders said it was coincidental, but it was bad timing for a startup that prides itself on reliability. Koum and Acton are so fixated on uptime that no one is allowed to talk to WhatsApp's server guys in the months before Christmas as they prepare for the message deluge. Visitors are rarely allowed into the office, lest they be a distraction. A whiteboard in the office shows the number of days since the last outage or incident, as a factory might show a tally for injuries or deaths. "A single message is like your firstborn child," said Acton, a new parent. "We can never drop a message." He pulled up a photo of his late stepfather, sent to his phone in April 2012. "This is why I hate Snapchat," where photos and messages disappear after viewing.

The dollars will start coming in greater numbers once WhatsApp can iron out dead-simple billing arrangements with wireless carriers. Koum doesn't want to risk putting users off with a complicated payment-request system and watch them run to free rivals. Right now, it charges only in the handful of countries where credit card penetration is high and mobile payments systems are culturally prevalent. Google is striking billing deals with carriers on behalf of all Android apps, but progress has been slow: Android carrier billing is available in just twenty-one countries, and to the ongoing chagrin of other developers, mobile payments still aren't standardized. Koum thinks the real money will start flowing by 2017 and beyond, at which point he plans to have 1 billion users. "We are very early in our monetization efforts," said Neeraj Arora, WhatsApp's business development manager. "Revenue is not important to us." Arora has brokered partnerships with about fifty carriers to prebundle the app into texting plans. It has also struck a noncommercial partnership with Nokia to put a WhatsApp button on the inexpensive Asha 210 phone.

Keeping people from switching to another service is another priority. The fear of losing eyeballs is what drove Zuckerberg to pay so dearly, and there's not much stopping them from leaving WhatsApp. "For the last five years WhatsApp has been exclusively focused on delivering 'SMS but free,' and they have done a great job at that. But at some point the user is going to move on," said Ted Livingston, a former BlackBerry engineer who founded the teen-friendly mobile messenger Kik. "This is why WhatsApp feels like BlackBerry to me. For years BlackBerry was exclusively focused on e-mail. But once the consumer understood this, they asked, 'What comes next?' The iPhone answered that question, and all of a sudden BlackBerry was left behind."

Koum is staying focused on keeping WhatsApp running and keeping users from going away. A couple of nights a month he pulls up to a nondescript cinder-block building in San Jose, grabs a gym bag, and walks into a dimly lit gym for a private boxing lesson with a gum-chewing coach standing next to a boom box blasting rap music. "He likes Kanye," said the coach, smiling, during one visit. He held two mitts up high as the six-foot-two Koum threw measured, powerful punches. Every few minutes Koum sat down for a break, slipping the gloves off and checking messages from Acton about WhatsApp's servers. Koum's style was very focused, the coach said. He doesn't want to get into kickboxing, like most other students, but just wants to get the punching right. You could make the same case for a certain messaging service that wants to be as straightforward as possible.

It's true, Koum said, ruddy-faced as he put on his socks and shoes. "I want to do one thing and do it well."